The Battle at Lindley's Mill

Stewart E. Dunaway

The Battle at Lindley's Mill
Copyright © All rights reserved
Stewart E. Dunaway

Second Edition – September 14, 2009

WWW.LULU.COM/Sedunaway

ISBN – 978-0-557-11531-0

(Below is a picture of the original marker placed at the battle site in 1915. A close up picture of this marker is on page 62. This marker is on the top of one of the ridges where the Patriot forces resided.)

Introduction	5
The History of the Mill	6
LINDLEY'S MILL	7
The Southern Campaign in the Revolutionary War	10
TIME-LINE	11
LOYALIST VERSUS PATRIOT	12
LOYALISTS	12
PRELUDE	17
New Governor	*17*
Fanning's Prelude	*18*
FANNING ATTACKS HILLSBOROUGH	20
THE BATTLE AT LINDLEY MILL	28
THE SECOND ATTEMPT – BROWN MARSH AND LIVINGSTON'S BRIDGE	41
Location – Brown Marsh	*42*
OFF TO WILMINGTON AND PRISON	49
AND THE OTHER PRISONERS?	52
Postlude	53
LIBERATE WILMINGTON?	53
GOVERNOR BURKE – RETURN TO OFFICE	54
COL ROBERT MEBANE	60
DAVID FANNING	60
Further Reading	64
Appendix A – Pension notes	65
Appendix B - Thomas Hart – Jesse Benton	70
Appendix C – Lindley History	73
LINDLEY FAMILY OVERVIEW	79
1750-1780	*81*
1780-1800	*82*
LAND DEED RECORDS	85
James Lindley Granville Grant #82 (1760)	*86*
James Lindley Granville Grant #153 (1760)	*88*
James Lindley Granville Grant (1760)	*90*
Thomas Lindley Granville Grant #66 (1759)	*93*
Hugh Laughlin Granville Grant #60 (1753)	*97*
Mill Specific (History)	*99*

Deed Records (Date Order) – 1755-1799 .... *101*
Deed Records (Date Order) – 1800-1809 .... *102*
Deed Records (Date Order) – 1810-1850 .... *103*
Deed Records (Lindley Grantee) *104*
Deed Records (Lindley Grantor) *105*

Index **107**

Introduction

The battle that occurred at Lindley's Mill is very unique. In North Carolina, the fight for independence occurred in (basically) two types of events. One that involved British Army and the American Army. The other deals with local Patriot Militia and the Loyalist Militia, or the Tories. This later situation involves citizen against fellow citizen, which is more of a civil war. Of course, there is much more involved between these two opposing parties, than will be discussed here. Never the less, they were opposing viewpoints with armed men, which will lead to bloodshed.

The Battle at Lindley's Mill was one such conflict (Tory vs. Patriot). This occurs on September of 1781, long after British Gen Lord Cornwallis, and his 2000+ British Army left the state, after the Battle of Guilford Courthouse. Lindley's Mill was not fought by British Redcoats. It was not a planned Patriot battle under the command of (Southern American Army), Gen Nathanael Greene. It was a local militia unit attempting to free the Governor, his staff, and fellow citizens taken prisoner by a Tory commander – David Fanning.

David Fanning is well known in North Carolina as a tenacious loyalist. He was enlisted and installed by the British. This book includes his enlistment order from British Maj. Craig. It authorized him to take up arms, form an army, and capture any rebel. A rebel? England considered the Colonist as rebelling against law and order. Thus they were rebellious and therefore rebels. Taking up arms against the King, as a colonist, was a serious crime. England had rejected diplomatic efforts, including the Declaration of Independence. This rebellious activity of the Colonist had to stop, and David Fanning was enlisted to assist in this effort. How? Destabilize the rebel government, their leaders, etc.

This book provides a detailed review of this event, as the result of my one year study and research in the life of Thomas Burke. His term as Governor of the State (3rd Governor) occurred during a very difficult time of war. Unfortunately, his service was interrupted when David Fanning took him prisoner. The British knew that without political leaders, the rebellion would end, and they really disliked Burke. He was a principle oriented man that disliked English rule. He served as one of the Congressmen from N.C. (Continental Congress) as well as representing the Hillsborough District during the early time of forming N.C. Provincial Congress. Burke became a prized target for Fanning (and the British).

Special thanks to *John and Judy Braxton,* and the *Lindley Family*, for their willingness to allow people access on their land to visit an important - historical location. I would like to note the kindness of *Travis Braxton*, during my many visits to Orange County Deed Office. He was well aware of his family history, and local history as well. I thoroughly enjoyed all my visits with him.

Stewart Dunaway

The History of the Mill

Lindley's Mill was established in 1755 (as a partnership) between Thomas Lindley and Hugh Laughlin.

Lindley's Mill

Thomas Lindley, son of James Lindley, and Eleanor Parke, was born in Ireland in 1706. He married Ruth Hadley, daughter of Simon Hadley at the New Garden Pennsylvania meeting of the Society of Friends October 21, 1731.

In the deed records (book 1, pg. 36) of Orange County, North Carolina is this agreement (August 10, 1755): "...***Hugh Laughlin, planter, on the one part and Thomas Lindley, on the other, have agreed to become partners in joint company to erect and build a water grist mill on Cane Creek, to the south side of Haw River. The water to be taken out of that land owned by Hugh Laughlin and the mill to be built on that part owned by Thomas Lindley, 3 and ¾ acres, Sep. Court 1755...***" Hugh Laughlin owned the land and river, up-stream and Lindley owned the land the mill was placed on, so this was a perfect business relationship.

The battle at Lindley's Mill was a difficult day for Thomas Lindley, as well as all families involved in the battle. Tragically, the Lindley family were split on which side to fight for. As a result of this, it pitted father against son, and brother against brother. Thomas Lindley was 75 years of age at the time of the battle. It is believed that he died that day in September, as a result of a heart attack, instigated by witnessing his family fighting amongst each other. After the battle, the women tended to the wounded at Thomas Lindley's home, as well as many others in the area, Tory or Whig, it did not matter. Thomas had a son (John Lindley) that served in the Revolutionary War as a Captain under Colonel David Fanning on the Tory side. In a letter from British Maj. James Craig (Wilmington headquarters) he writes David Fanning (who is recovering from his wounds from the battle) Oct. 13, 1781, "...***The circumstance of the circumstances of the Stallion you mention, I determined it in your favor and took him away from Mr. Campbell, or rather, from a gentleman to whom he sold him, he has been with my horses ever since and never rode, I now send him to you by Captain Linley.***" Thomas also had another son (Jonathan) who fought with the Patriots, and yet another son, (James) already dead from a battle in South Carolinas – serving as a Tory.

The Lindley family illustrates the struggle, and the difficulty, borne by many families in North Carolina during the fight for America's Independence.

(Pictured on the left is the present day Mill building).

(Here is another picture of the mill site, which has some of the original parts, although no longer used. The mill today grinds organic grain.)

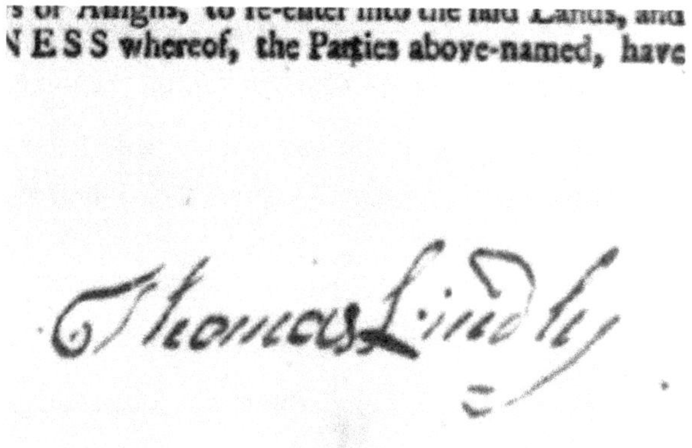

Thomas Lindley's actual signature on his Granville Grant (1759). (Note: Lindley without the "e")

Below is Hugh Laughlin's signature from his land grant (1753).

James Lindley's signature from his grant (1760).

The Lindley family donated the land (5.5 acres) for the Spring Meeting House. This location (cemetery) contains the Lindley family cemetery.

Pictured on the right is the cemetery across the road from the Spring Meeting House.

On the left is a marker for Thomas Lindley and wife Ruth.

Here (right) is a marker for William Braxton.

The Southern Campaign in the Revolutionary War

North Carolina was part of the "Southern Campaign" devised by Gen. Clinton, Commander of the British forces in America. His attempt was to gather the strong loyalist support of the Carolinas and then take Virginia and attack Gen. George Washington to win the war. He will appoint Gen Cornwallis as the commander of the Southern Campaign, while Clinton focuses on the Northern effort against Gen. Washington. In turn, Gen Washington will enlist the services (after replace Gen Gates) of Gen Nathanael Greene to take charge of Patriot forces against Gen Cornwallis.

Lindley's Mill, is not part of the Southern Campaign, technically speaking. However, until the British surrender in October 19, 1781 at the Battle at Yorktown, the Southern Campaign was still in operation. Thus my reason for including an overview of this timeline, and the events that occurred during it.

Time-Line

The Southern Campaign started with the capture of Charles Town (Charleston), South Carolina as Gen Charles Cornwallis and his two officers, Lieutenant Col. Banastre Tarleton, and Lieutenant Col. Patrick Ferguson, began to move into the Carolinas. Charles Town was a very important sea port, and controlling this location was crucial to the British movement inland. Here are the battles listed in chronological order, including both Carolinas:

- Charles Town – March 29-May 12, 1780
- Waxhaws – May 29, 1780
- Musgrove Mill – August 18, 1780
- Camden – August 16, 1780
- King's Mountain – October 7, 1780
- Cowpens – January 17, 1781
- Race to the Dan – February 13, 1781
- Hart's Mill – February 22, 1781
- Pyle's Defeat – February 24, 1781
- Clapp's Mill – March 2, 1781
- Weitzel's Mill – March 6, 1781
- Guilford Courthouse – March 15, 1781
- Hobkirk's Hill – April 25, 1781
- Eutaw Springs – September 8, 1781
- **Lindley's Mill – September 13, 1781**
- Yorktown – October 19, 1781

Since South Carolina's most populous and important town (Charles Town) was now under British control, the next move was to go into North Carolina and take control of this important state. Cornwallis was faced with a large task, since North Carolina had a much larger area to contend with, and unbeknownst to him, a lot more resistance. The British, and their superior Navy, took control of North Carolina's main sea port, Wilmington. Yet, the inland battle will take its toll on the Brits. The assumption was that loyalist support (those citizens that continued to support the King and remain loyal) in the Carolinas was much greater than in the other colonies. But this was not true, and Cornwallis did not enlist many loyalist supporters as expected as they continue to battle American opposition (referred to by the British as – rebels).

As you can see from the above time-line, Lindley's Mill occurred very close to the end of the war, and as you will soon read, was not really part of the British Military effort. This was another battle between residents of the state, Tory versus Whig. At this point in time, Cornwallis was in Virginia, soon to catch the wrath of General Washington and the French at Yorktown, which ultimately ends the war.

Loyalist versus Patriot

Whigs or Patriots were those residents who sided for independence from English rule. The Loyalist or Tory was a resident that remained loyal to the Crown, and actually fought with or for the British side of the war. In some instances there were family divisions, brothers fighting brothers, and certainly neighbor against neighbor. In the northern colonies this was more like a political view, such as a democrat versus a republican viewpoint. Opposing views, just not worth killing each other over. True to the point, Major General Nathanael Greene, the American commander in North Carolina, (replacing Gen. Gates in 1781), seeing both sides (he served Gen Washington in the North before taking charge of the Southern Campaign) has this interesting comment "[Carolina citizens]...*were the most unhappy and frustrated he had ever encountered. The bitterness between patriot and Loyalist far exceeded in physical antagonism anything he had ever seen in the eastern or middle states.*" He continued "*...the difference between Whig and Tory is little more than a division of sentiment, but here they persecute each other with little less than savage fury....the sufferings and distress of the inhabitants beggars all description, and required the liveliest imagination to conceive the cruelties and devastations which prevail.*" (See Caty – A Biography of Catherine Littlefield Greene - pg. 85)

The decision to remain loyal or rebel was not an easy one. It is a very complex situation, and involves deeply educated ideals with ties to religion. Therefore, this book is not written to criticize either side, but to highlight the differences and how they were involved in the Revolutionary War.

Loyalists

Col. David Fanning (greatly feared by the inhabitants) was a "loyalist" that being, loyal to the Crown, siding with the British, against the rebellion of the Colonists. Loyalists who took up arms were known as a Tory. The reader should be aware of the differences between a Tory, and a British solider. British military (also known as British Regular or Redcoat) were well trained soldiers, sent to America to fight for the King. Tories, were like all "militia", just armed residents taking the opposing side (for Independence). During the American Revolution, both Tory and British Army fought in North Carolina (especially in the Orange County area).

David Fanning wrote a book "**The Narrative of Colonel David Fanning**" published in 1865, where he details *his opinion* of what he accomplished during the war. He said he was 19 years old when he entered the war effort in 1775. He also stated that he felt, "**Rebellion according to Scripture is, as the Sin of witchcraft; and the propagators thereof, has more than once punished; ...**". This clearly documents Fanning held a religious view, possibly justifying his tenacious style (religious based war tends to be more vicious).

> **Militia vs. Continental or Army**
>
> Patriot militia men were enlisted for brief tours of duty (up to 3 months). This allowed them to return to their farms and families. They could serve several times, if so called.
>
> Continental men were enlisted for the duration of the war. They were trained in military combat procedures better (typically) than the militia. Yet, this does not infer the militia was ineffective. The Overmountain men (King's Mountain, October 1780) would be considered militia, and executed their efforts with deadly precision.

David's life story is a mix of facts and tales, which can be difficult to separate. He was a resident of Virginia, and owned a plantation of his own, and one he inherited from his father. Born October 25, 1755 in Amelia County, Virginia, *tradition* states he was about six years old when his dad (David Sr.), died. However, in a document from the Public Record Office (PRO) in England, an affidavit (NC Archives # 77.153.1) states that his father died in 1775. The year 1775 coincides with his entrance into the war. Also this date (year) seems to be more plausible (as opposed to his dad dieing when David was a child), as Edmund Fanning said that (or inferred that he knew) he knew David's father and family (which would require a much later year, due to Edmunds age). Never the less, the *story* continues, that his father died by drowning in the Deep River (in North Carolina) whilst looking for suitable land to move his family. As a young boy he became a foster child, and lived a very difficult and dirty life, thus having a rather nasty disease contracted on his scalp. This in turn festered and smelled poorly (people couldn't stand to be near him due to the stench), which supposedly cause total hair loss. He wore a scarf on his head, or, as some stories state, he wore a wig (most believe a scarf). David ultimately finds another family to care for him, and they cure his disease, although he never regains his natural hair. *No document, affidavit, memorial, nor anything in writing, can confirm this story.* Yet, it seems all the records from England, documents his father's death in 1775.

Another "memorial" from the PRO records (NC Archives 77.153.1-2) states (1787), **"...So early as November 1775 he took arms under Col Robinson in S. Carolina when the Rebels were dispersed at 96. During the course of the two following years he was much harassed and then imprisoned and once tried for life. In 1779 he was under the necessity of doing duty for some months in the Rebel Militia but upon arrival of the British troops in So. Carolina he immediately joined them and served in the militia with the British Army until Feb 1781 when he was sent into No. Carolina for the purpose of embodying the militia of that province. In July 1781 he received an appointment of Col. Of the Randolph and Chatham Co. Militia and in consequence embodied nearly 1000 men with whom he marched to Hillsborough and there surprised and took prisoner Gov Thomas Burke with his Couriers and a considerable No. Carolina Continental Officers and men all of whom were conducted safe to Wilmington but Col Fanning had the misfortune to be severely wounded in his retreat from Hillsborough by which being considered unable to travel he was obliged to remain some months concealed in the words..."** Then towards the end it states, **"...Col Fanning says that he had some property left him in Virginia by his Father who died in 1775..."**. This is the only document which provides a great overview of his beginning activity in South Carolina, prior to his move into North Carolina. What stories could originate from being a fellow patriot militia man, then cross over into the enemies lines, and fight against the cause!

November 1786 David Fanning files a pension in Canada for the loss of his property in America (PRO AO 13 – ERD/7674). His preamble is interesting, *"…who uniformity and religiously adhered to his duty and loyalty to the best of sovereign for which he suffered persecution and many other inconveniences….commanded from one to nine hundred fifty men and engaged in six and thirty skirmishes in North Carolina and four in South Carolina,….twice wounded and fourteen times a prisoner…"* Here is his "schedule" of losses:

- 550 acres of land in Amelia County Virginia where on was a dwelling house and other out houses; part of it consisted of a large apple and peach orchard, and had other large and useful improvements - £687.10.0

- 550 acres of land near the above, with a dwelling house and other improvements claimed in light as heir at law to the estate of his late father - £412.10.0

- 3 saddle horses – £40.0.0

- 12 plantation horses and three colts - £96.0.0

- Debts on bonds notes etc. – £289.0.0

- 5 Negro slaves – £100.0.0

Total loss - £1625.0.0

David Fanning's life's history will not be fully discussed in this book. However, it will be important to address his last name, since Hillsborough has another Fanning in history – Edmund Fanning. Edmund Fanning was well known in Orange County, during the Regulation movement in the late 1760's. He resided in Hillsborough, and was very close to Royal Governor William Tryon. Edmund was not closely related to David, yet we have to assume, that somewhere back in the family tree, they are related. True to this fact, a rare letter written by Edmund Fanning, addressed to David Fanning, highlights the possibility of a closer family tie, than most historian infer.

Here is the letter (PRO X/J 6385 – Archives – 76.2367.1) in question, and *note the very last line*:

Charles Town 29th Sep 1781

Dear Sir,

All the caused required of the bearer I take the liberty of commending him to you for to be employed with you as an officer to an officers in Governor Martins Crops, but he tells me that rather serve with you among his old acquaintances in short I honor Mr. James Munro to be a deserving officer and recommend him to you as such, and as my Friend, as my old brother officer Col Hector McNeal is dead I desire your attention and Friendship to Mr. Munro who can tell you how I am and how sincerely proud and rejoiced I am at hearing of your Loyal and brave conduct and that of my good old friends the Loyal Militia of North Carolina under your command. I desire to kindly remembered to them all and have with them glory and success, I do assure you that I should be greatly rejoiced if I was ordered to join and help our Loyal friends in North Carolina with my Regiment. I shall write to you again before long, but in the mean time I should be very happy to receive a line from you or any of my North Carolina friends with you and would be obliged to you if you would present my compliments to them all. If your Father is still alive I desire you would present my compliment to him and tell him that I hope to see him and Family and all my old acquaintances before long, and am with sincere regard and esteem

Dear Sir

Your most obedient Humble Servant

Edmund Fanning

James Munro was a well known loyalist residing in Hillsborough. In fact, he destroyed three volumes of deed records, which continue to impact historical research (specific details) to this day. The comment about David's father could have been a simple expression of respect, and not that that Edmund knew his father. However, you cannot discount the possibility that Edmund knew his parental background. Historians state that David Fanning's father drowned when he was a young child. If Edmund did know his dad, then historians are wrong.

What was Fanning up to in North Carolina, during the war? The British had complete control in Wilmington, and Major James Craig enlisted the services of David Fanning, and his men, to "stir the pot", and create havoc and disorder in an attempt to undermine the Patriot cause. This Fanning did very well. In addition, he was supplied with the necessary goods by the British, very scarce supplies. He and his men traveled the state killing, and capturing people who were against the Crown.

The Battle at Lindley Mill

The Battle of Lindley Mill occurred in order to free the Governor of North Carolina, as well as other people captured in Hillsborough, N.C. This was not a military campaign in the purest sense, but more of a rescue mission. (Note: the map {1770} below was drawn prior to the road continuing past the mill site.)

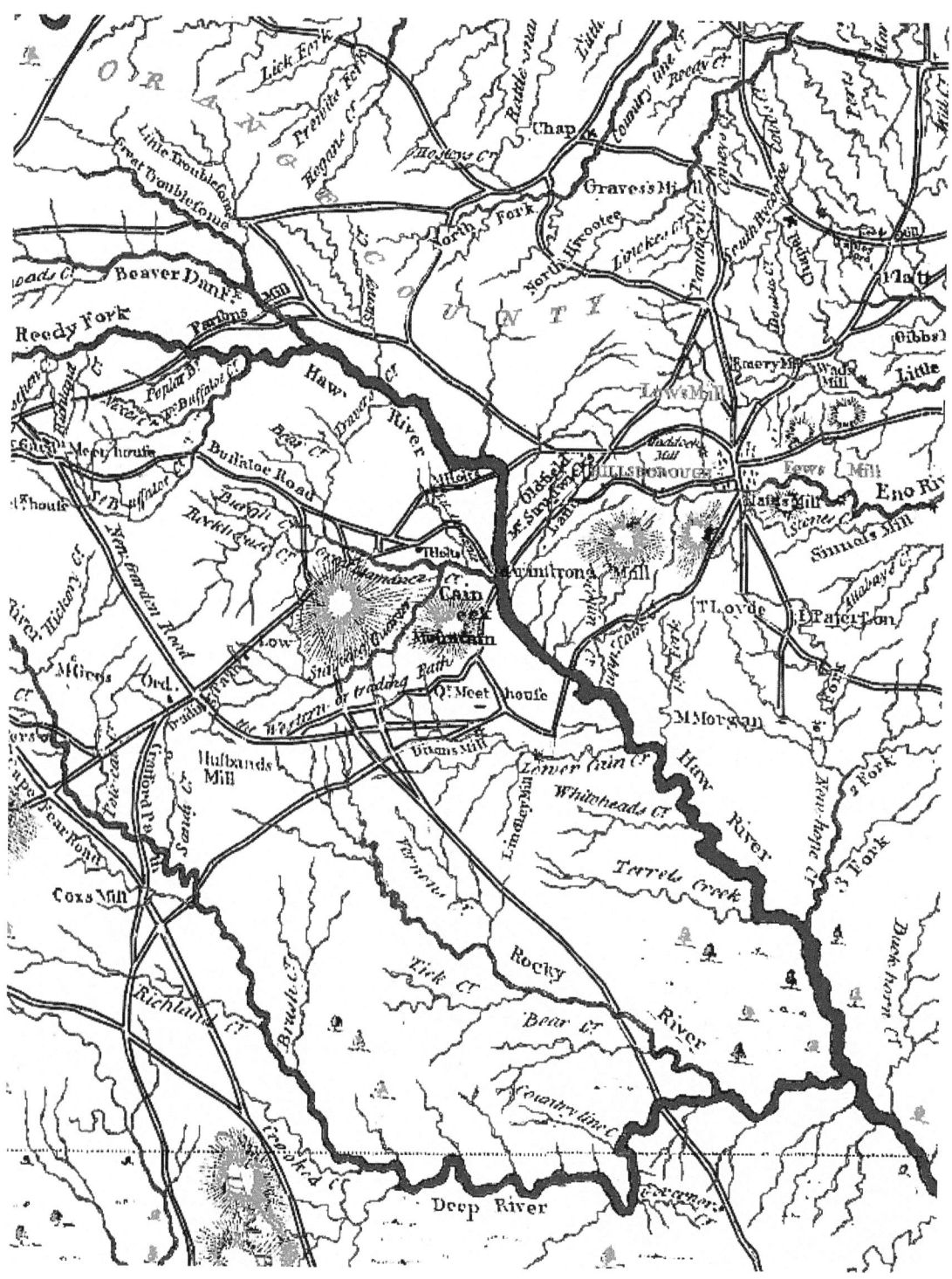

Prelude

Before we begin with the main subject of this booklet, let's review some events prior to the battle.

New Governor

On June 25, 1781 the General Assembly elected Dr. Thomas Burke of Hillsborough, N.C. to be third Governor of the state. Prior to being governor, he served in Congress, as well as early Provincial Congress of North Carolina, and was a practicing lawyer. After his election, Thomas Burke was traveling between Hillsborough and New Bern. Just prior to his capture he was located at the Nutbush Church (former Church of England) for several months, located in Williamsborough, Granville County. A Tavern located across from the Church was the location where officials met, and discussed current events. Gov. Burke was attempting to enlist the help of the people in North Carolina, primarily in supplying goods for the war effort, which were sorely lacking at this time. Based on numerous letters, Burke was also heavily engaged in the war, directing the militia, and providing any intelligence he came upon (enemy movement and location). (Note: Nutbush Church remains standing to this day, pictured here. Unfortunately the Tavern is in great decay.)

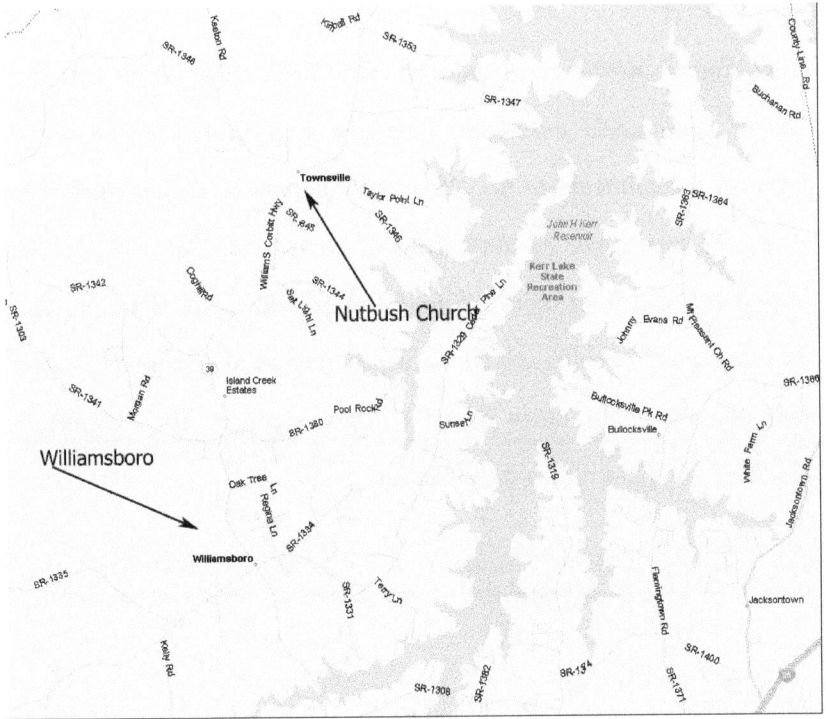

The modern road map on the left shows the location of the church, as well as old Williamsboro. Flooding of Nutbush Creek has covered up the old roadways from the 18th century.

Burke returns to Hillsborough on September 9th writing several letters on the 10th and 11th, mainly to Gen Butler about the enemy's movement as well as Fanning's location.

James Iredell accompanied Thomas Burke on his travels to Hillsborough, and then on to Salisbury. However, at Williamsborough (Granville Co,) he wrote his wife (September 11) and said he was very ill.

Thomas Burke, "*most obligingly furnished me with tartar, and prepared it for me. Three different days I took it…*" showing Thomas didn't drop his doctor skills along the way. Never the less, James remained too ill to travel. Then in a letter to his wife (Hannah) dated September 16, 1781 he wrote "*I wrote you two or three days ago, acquainting you of my having been sick here, but then being recover, and I thank God I still continue perfectly well. My sickness I at the time deemed a great misfortune, but I consider it far otherwise now, for in all human probability, nothing else prevented Col. Williams and myself sharing a very melancholy fate which now attends the Governor.*" (more of this letter to follow) Note: James Iredell becomes a Supreme Court Judge. (See *Life and Correspondence of James Iredell Vol 1* for more about Iredell)

Fanning's Prelude

David Fanning received his commission from British Major James Craig on July 5, 1781. Here is the exact transcript (from PRO records):

By James Henry Craig Esq. Major in His Majesty's 82nd Regiment commanding a detachment of the Kings Forces in North Carolina.

To David Fanning Esq.

These are to appoint you to be Colonel of the Loyal Militia of Randolph and Chatham Counties who are directed to obey you as such in all lawful commands whatever, and you are authorized to grant commissions to the necessary persons of known attachments to his Majesty's person and Government to Act as Captains and Subalterns to the different companies of the militia aforesaid. As Colonel you are hereby fully empowered to assemble [damaged] and lead them against any parties of Rebels or other the Kings enemies as often as necessary to compel all persons whatever to join you or to seize and disarm and when necessary detain in confinement all Rebels or other persons acting against His Majesty's Government to do all other acts becoming a Kings Officer and a good subject.

Given at Wilmington this 5th July 1781

David Fanning will become a very important asset for the British effort in North Carolina. His assignment was well documented above. However, he was really focusing on destabilization of the governmental infrastructure of the State, than a military effort. To be clear, Fanning and his men were not a military force, or he would have focused strictly on military battles, like the Royal N.C. Regiment under Col. John Hamilton (supporting Gen Cornwallis during the Southern Campaign). Yet, you cannot ignore that Patriot Militia would battle with him, as we will witness later in this book. If you research Fanning's activity, focusing on who he is targeting, you will find public officials (i.e. Mayor etc.), and militia leaders that were supporting the resistance movement. During Fanning's last month in N.C., he will be found executing people, more so than involved in "battles" or skirmishes with the Patriot militia.

David Fanning with his men, were not idle. In fact they were in several battles prior to this attack on Hillsborough. These two battles were known as the Battle at Beatti's (Bettis and Bettie) Bridge, and the other, Battle of Kirk's Farm.

August 26, 1781, David Fanning, Col McNeil, and Col Slingsbee were in Bladen County, near Wilmington, with the Patriot forces under Col Thomas Wade in hot pursuit. Col Wade had about 400 men, while Fanning enlisted just over 220. As each side were taking their positions, Fanning and his men were more strategically placed, although outnumbered almost 2 to 1. By 11 o'clock September 1, the battle begins, and the first shots fired were by the Patriot forces, which brought down eighteen loyalists and their horses. The Tories dismounted, and advanced up a hill after the patriots. Like King's Mountain, those on top (the patriots in this instance) were shooting over their heads below. However, on the reverse side, when a person on the hill rises up, those below easily targeted them. Ultimately the patriot forces give in, and retreat into another trap as they crossed the Lumber River where Col McNeil was waiting for them. As the patriot forces fought through this situation, they were able to flee, although pursued by Fanning for seven miles. Patriot losses were high, as Fanning reported 54 prisoners and 23 dead. Here was a stunning victory for the Loyalist cause in just under two hours of fighting. On the Loyalist side there were just a few wounded or dead.

Fanning's force return to their headquarters at Cox's Mill (located in Eastern Randolph County) arriving September 9. It was at this time that Fanning was starting to plan his attack on Hillsborough. They were gathering intelligence reports as to the whereabouts of Gen Butler, who was still at Ramsey's Mill. On the morning of September 11 they start marching towards Hillsborough. Fanning also learned (via intel) there was a small force of about 25 men roaming around Orange County. Fanning dispatched the loyalist force in Orange County under Capt. Richard Edwards to find and attack this small band of Patriots under the command of Allen and Young. They were found at Kirk's Farm where the loyalists ambushed the Patriots. Both Captain Allen and Young were wounded, and Capt Edwards was killed as well as 10 other loyalist who were left on the field. Caruthers remarked, nothing more is known about the Patriot side. However, a letter from Jesse Benton of Hillsborough to Thomas Hart (dated September 29, 1781) provided more details about the battle. *"**Capt Abrm Allen with 50 men had a battle lately with Dick Edwards & his Company killed Edwards & 4 or 5 more. Allen*** *got shot through the body tho will get well, Lt Jos Young & 2 privates killed on our side.*" The remaining band of Loyalist head towards Hillsborough to rejoin Fanning' main force.

> **Jesse Benton & Thomas Hart** – Jesse Benton moved from Granville County to Hillsborough around 1770 where he practiced law. Thomas Hart, a local resident of Hillsborough joined and fought with Gov. Tryon (against the Regulators) in the War of the Regulation (1771). This is how Thomas received the title Colonel, not from the Revolutionary War. Thomas never served in the War for Independence. He purchased Maddox's Mill on the Eno (1.5 miles west of Hillsborough). Hart leaves the state, as he dislikes the unrest he sees, during the transition away from British Rule towards Independence. I would categorize Hart as "neutral" towards the Revolution. He developed a large plantation and business, known as Hartford. This was built around the Maddox Mill complex. Jesse Benton resides at Hartford. He becomes Hart's attorney whilst Thomas moves to Maryland and then on to Kentucky. Benton was very active in his legal practice, town politics, and running the mill complex. Jesse's brother was Samuel Benton, County Clerk for a number of years in Hillsborough.

The following letter from Jesse Benton (Sep 29, 1781) is so valuable, as it was written in a timely manner. He expressed his views of the "current state of the union" in a letter to Thomas Hart (a former land owner and citizen of Hillsborough) – "*I am very glad you got away from here [document damaged] time you did; for had you remained, [document damaged] convinced your moveable property would have been plundered from you, & yourself a prisoner, as had lately been the case with a great number of our best men. Our state has really become odious, owing (I am afraid) to mismanagement in the Legislative or Executive powers a small party of British, not exceeding 400, have been in Wilmington ever since last winter, have had free communication with the Tories in the country, & meeting with no opposition have made them so formidable that the state is next to being reduced. One David Fanning (an old horse thief) & Hector McNeil have kidnap'd almost every leading man between here & Wilmington*"

Fanning Attacks Hillsborough

Gov. Burke was in route to Salisbury, to visit that area of the state (probably to visit Col James C. Mountflorence – State Quartermaster in Salisbury dist.), but planned a short visit in his home town, Hillsborough. In a letter from Mr. Armstrong on September 3, 1781 he wrote Gov. Burke, "*I had your furniture brought into Town in a most shattered Condition, your Trunks unlocked, your Desk and Bookcase very much Hurt, your papers in a great measure loose; but I still hope nothing is lost, I have put them into the House where you intend living where thy are very far from being secure there being no keys to the Doors; this induced me to consent that some officers might go into the House so that a sentinel may be kept at the Door.*" He continues, "*It was not with Cheerfulness that Mr. Allison let me have the House, as he says Mr. Tatum did not settle anything respecting the rent with him according to your promise.*" This letter proves that he was renting a home in town, and not staying at his plantation, known as Tyaquin (two miles north of downtown). Prior articles on this subject leave the location of Burke (at the time of the attack) inconclusive. Researching Mr. Allison (in an attempt to locate what house he was renting) only uncovered his occupation being in real estate. The precise home (by lot number) has not been determined.

Just before his attack on Hillsborough Fanning wrote, "*The day following, I arrived at Coxe's Mill, where I issued the following advertisement; and circulated it through the country;*

Advertisement

This is to let all persons know, that do not make ready and repair immediately to camp, that their property shall be seized and sold at public sale; and if they are taken, and brought into camp they shall be sent to Wilmington, as prisoners, and there remain, as such, in the provost; and be considered Rebels; also, if any rebel is willing to surrender and come in he shall reap the benefit of a subject.

David Fanning,
Col'o Com'g loyal Militia
Camp Coxe's Mill, 6th Sept., 1781.

David Fanning provided the detail about his forces (which varied in size). He writes, "***On the 9th of Sept. I was joined by Col'n McDugald of the Loyal Militia of Cumberland County, with 200 men; and Col. Hector McNiel, with his party from Bladen of 70 men; and in consequence of my advertisement I had also 435, who came in; and many found me afterwards. I had previously determined within myself to take the Rebel, Governor Burke of North Carolina and I had a conversation with Major Craigg, on that subject. I now thought it a favorable opportunity, as I found myself at the head of 950 men of my own regiment; exclusive of McDuglad and McNiel's regiments. I acquainted Major Raines, of my resolution, who approved of it.***"

As you can see, he did not always operate as an independent entity, as some authors allude to, but had discussed his plans with British authorities. David Fanning was aware that Gen Butler and Col Robert Mebane were in the general area, but Fanning decided not to fight them, instead headed towards Hillsborough. He states how he proceeded thus, "***I pushed all that day and the following night; at 7 o'clock on the morning of the 12th***

we entered the town in three divisions, and received several shots from different houses; however we lost none and suffered no damage, except one man wounded." Jesse Benton provided the following information about the Tory and Patriot locations prior to entering Hillsborough, "***This said Fanning & McNeil had hovered about the Buffalo Ford on Deep River two or three weeks preceding this accident with their men embodied; Gen Butler & Col Robt***

Mebane with 200 horse & 100 foot had been 5 or 6 days near Crows Ford on Haw River to watch their motions however the Tories executed their designs."

Governor Burke thought Fanning was going to initially attack Gen. Butler on the Haw River, "*The enemy, disappointed in their enterprise, pursued towards Hillsborough in hopes of falling in with him on their march, were informed by their connections in and about Hillsborough that I was there with little or no forces, and they instantly made their object, forgetting, or perhaps not knowing the danger of leaving General Butler with a force in their rear, for which Ignorance or neglect they suffered very severely on their retreat, and were very near being utterly routed.*" Only Burke identifies Fanning's mistake.

Then Gov. Burke continues with the capture, "*A dark night and foggy Morning with the neglect of the patrols who were ordered on the roads leading to the Town, enabled them to invest in the surrounding woods, and a little after sunrise about five hundred entered on all sides. We were in no condition to engage. We had few or no effective Arms, and but few men, even including the Townsmen, who were all peaceably in their houses, and no number was in one place collected. A scattering fire was for some little time kept up, but my house soon became the principle object. To escape was impracticable and resistance was in vain, yet the savage manners and appearance of the men made me expect nothing but massacre, and I preferred dying, sword in hand, than yielding to their barbarity. Thus resolved attended by Cap. Reid, my aid-de-camp, Mr. Huske, my Secretary, and an orderly Sergeant of the Continental Service, and armed only with our swords and pistols, we sustained for some time a close and hot fire, until at length Capt. Reid went through their fire and brought a gentleman in uniform of a British Officer up to me to whom, after repeated assurances of proper treatment, I gave up my sword.*" This letter identifies a British officer being with Fanning's Tories. Was this planned (possible negotiator)? Burke recognized the different states of mind in dealing with a "crowd" of angry

men, as opposed to regular British military rules of engagement. He then continues, "*This gentleman had much difficulty afterwards to preserve us from the violence of the men, but being joined by some Highland gentlemen whom I had formerly made prisoners and remembered that they had been treated with humanity, they were at length able to cover us from the fury of our assailants. Thus I became a prisoner, …*."

David Fanning stated, "*We killed fifteen of the rebels, and wounded twenty; and took upwards of two hundred prisoners ; amongst them was the Governor, his Council, and part of the Continental Colonels, several captains and subalterns, and seventy one continental soldiers out of a church. We proceeded to the Goal (jail), and release thirty Loyalists, and British soldiers; one of which, was to have been hanged on that day.*" Fanning gathered more than just the Governor, his staff, and military men, but included some citizens in the town. There isn't any historical documentation to sustain that citizens had died by the hands of Fanning's men, as Fanning stated (15 killed). Neither are there any documented stories from Hillsborough citizens about being a prisoner of Fanning's, except Gov. Burke, his staff, and the soldiers in town that day. As a historical reference, the 1790 census of North Carolina has 40 "heads of household" in the city of Hillsborough and 187 in the Hillsborough District. It is plausible that Fanning's prisoner count was about 100 prisoners, of

which, 70 were the militia, and the 30 other would be Burke, his staff, and some residents, not the whole town. There is a commonly quoted story about Tories harassing James Hogg, and trying to steal the silver buckles from his shoes. They did not capture or harm him, and other residents remained unmolested (i.e. Jesse Benton). That said, Thomas Burke mentioned in a letter (while in captivity on James Island) "peaceable inhabitants" were captured, documenting that some civilians were incarcerated. *The 200 count is overly stated by Fanning.* Yet, history books continue to re-tell this story, using David's account.

Thanks to a pension, Jacob Rich (#W26380) stated that his men were encamped about one mile away from town and heard the battle and, "*…marched hastily to the relief of the place and then became engaged with the enemy who had a superior force. Our company was all killed or taken prisoners except five. I was wounded in the hip, having received two balls in the right hip…*" He then continues, "*I fortunately was able to get to my horse and was aided in making my escape by my friend and brother soldier Joseph M. Adams.*" Here is the only known record of any effort by patriot forces in Hillsborough. This pension finally identifies who were the 15 people killed by Fanning during this battle. Therefore it was Patriot militia, and not local citizens shooting from their homes. Jacob said that he was a Lieutenant in the militia and was under the command of

Capt John McClennen (probably John Clendenin). He mentions that McClennen was recently taken a prisoner, put on parole. However, he broke parole, and gathered a group of volunteers, of which Jacob was a member. Other records document McClennen as being captured in Eutaw Springs. This pension verifies he was a prisoner, however, he was paroled. Another pension application (#S17304) of an Orange County resident, Robert Burnside, states that he was with Capt John Clendenin and was captured at Hillsboro. *"…we marched through Orange County N.C. to the relief of Hillsborough which was put in the hands of a Col McNeil commandant of the Tories…our Captain [John Clendenin] pushed into town [Hillsborough] where we were fired upon and after compelled to give way this applicant was thrown by his horse and taken prisoner and put in jail but broke from there the same night…"*. These two pensions are important in documenting the attack on Hillsborough, as well as defining who fought the Tories.

Jesse Benton's letter (ibid) to Thomas Hart states, *"The last stroke they made was the 12th of this month when they came into Hillsborough at 7 O'Clock in the morning with 500 Tories killed five or six of the guard, took the Governor, several gentlemen inhabitants of the Town, Continentals & Militia troops, amounting in the whole to 140 odd men; made a general Jail delivery by setting at liberty about 40, Criminal, Deserters & Delinquents, whom they armed with our public muskets, & have since carried the prisoners safe into Wilmington, all except about a dozen who got paroled & escaped on the way."* Here is another account of just 150 prisoners.

Of the soldiers that were captured in Hillsborough, Col John Mebane, Col Alexander Mebane, and William Kinchen were fairly well documented. Local stories mention that Alexander Mebane escaped through the tall grass in the road which allowed him to notify Col Robert Mebane and Gen John Butler of what just occurred. Then Butler and Mebane gathered their troops together to battle the Tories at a strategic location they felt would give them an advantage, due to being outnumbered by almost 2 to 1. In a letter from Gen Greene to Col William R. Davie (Oct. 18, 1781) documents Davie's involvement, *" I congratulate you upon our happy prospects in Virginia, and upon your happy escape the other day in Hillsborough when Gov Burke and his suite were made prisoners."* The footnote to this entry in *Nathanael Greene Papers*, Vol. 9 stated that Col Davie's actual location is unknown and referenced a book *"Davie"* by Robinson (pg 120-121).

Col. Archibald Lytle was in charge of the 6th N.C. Regiment stationed in Hillsborough. It is assumed that it was Lytle's men (the 70 Continentals that were in the church) who were captured. From a letter written to Gen Greene by Col Lytle on December 27, 1781, he provides some insight to his role in this mess, and the following quote includes notes from the editors of *Nathanael Greene Papers*, Vol 10; **"He was taken prisoner when the British captured Charleston and was paroled on June 26, 1781. While still on parole, he was made a prisoner again, along with Gov. Burke and others, by a Banditti headed by a Mr. Fanning. At the time of his capture, Lytle's baggage, sidearms, and horses were plundered and his papers destroyed."** (the continuation of this letter will follow in another section)

There isn't a complete list of prisoners, however, a footnote in the *Nathanael Greene Papers*, states that **"A memo signed by Martin, which apparently accompanied his letter to Nathanael Greene, lists some of the Continental and militia officers and private citizens who had been captured with Burke."** The footnote references, University of Michigan - William Clements Library - as the source, but provided no details. Yet, it continues to confirm three "classifications" (Continental, Militia, and Citizen) of people taken prisoner. Below is a table listing all prisoners that filed a pension:

Albright	Henry	Prisoner	Capt James Trousdale, Lieu John Campbell - prison ship abt 11mnths - July 1782
Allen	William	Prisoner	Archibald Lytle, exchanged 8/11/1782 - on a ship
Allman	Edward	Prisoner	Gave no information
Austin	Benjamin	Prisoner	Capt. Abraham Allen, Col Hugh Teenan, escaped during transfer of prisons Apr 9, 1782
Christmas	Richard	Prisoner	Prison ship Eske, exch for Capt. Osbourn July 1, 1782
Fox	Gatus	Prisoner	Lytle, prisoner for 3 mths, sent to prison - "Provo"
Matthews	John	Prisoner	He said that he was captured "on their way" and McKay parolled him before Wilmington
McCauley	Matthew	Prisoner	Lieu Archibald Lytle - 6 months on Eske
Mebane	John	Prisoner	Prison Ship for several weeks exch for Lieu McClain
Neese	George	Prisoner	Capt John Clendenin, Wilmington to Eske to Charleston - July 1782 release
Turner	James	Prisoner	Taken across Woody's Ferry, then to Stallworth, then Lindley's, then on Eske

Here is a map that shows Gov. Burke's home ("X") in relation to downtown Hillsborough.

Jesse Benton's letter (ibid) continues about the activity after the capture (about Fanning leaving Hillsborough), and it documents a completely different account of what transpires, he writes, "*About 100 of the neighbors under the command of Col Tho Taylor pursued the Tories the evening of the 12th instant (myself in company) with a resolution to surprise their camp by night, but were so unfortunate as not to find the main body until after sunrise, tho, we passed them six miles and followed a party of about 100 (which were not the object of our attention at the time.) When we discovered the main camp near James Tinnens we were in imminent danger, & retreated to Hillsborough where we got reinforced, foraged & pursued again. In the course of the night we dispatched three men to find Genl Butler which they effected a little before day & gave him the first account of what has happened..*" Interesting that he states about "*100 of the neighbors*", this also proves that all of Hillsborough was not captured. It also has a differing story as to how Butler was notified.

Quickly, David Fanning and his band of men, along with his prisoners, left Hillsborough on their way to Wilmington, and since I-40 was not built, the road to Wilmington first went southwest towards Lindley Mill on Cane Creek, before turning south-eastwardly to Wilmington. David Fanning states, *"About 12o'clock, I left Hillsboro; and proceeded Eighteen Miles that night towards Coxe's Mill ; in the morning I pursed my march about Eight miles further, to Lindley's Mill on Cane Creek ; where Gen Butler and a party of rebels had concealed themselves."*

Below is a map (Strother's 1808) that illustrates the possible route (a number of roads to choose from). Several pension records mention Woody's Ferry as a crossing point. This was a well known route to Cross Creek (Fayetteville) or Wilmington. The road from Woody's Ferry, eventually fords Mary's Creek, and passes the Quaker Meeting House. Finally it winds its way to the ford on Cane Creek, near Lindley's Mill.

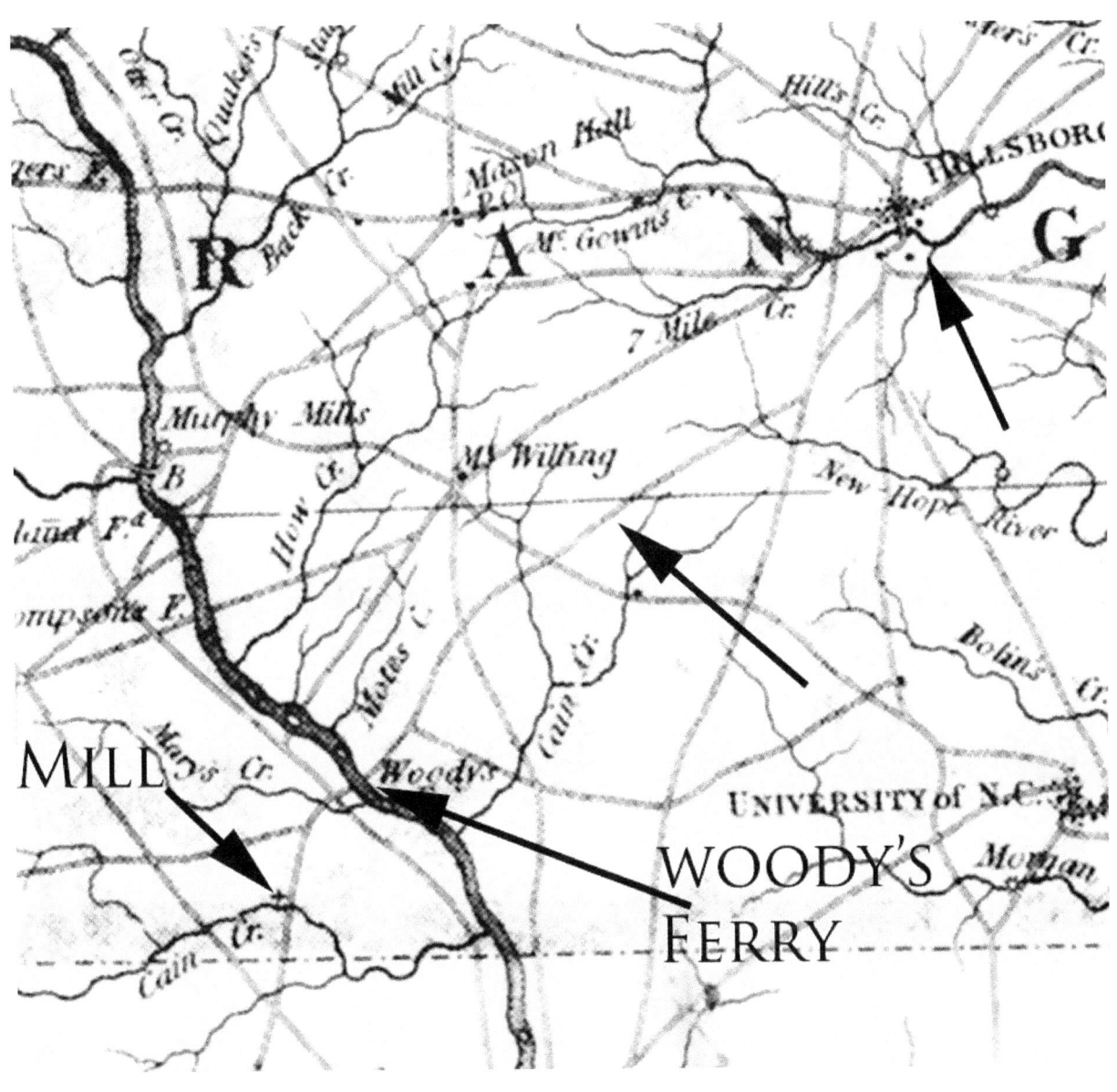

The Battle at Lindley Mill

As this large group of Tories (and prisoners) marched south, you have to picture how this occurred. It is assumed two columns (man side by side) with men in the front, prisoners in the middle, men in arrears. Spacing six feet between the men, and two columns, (950 men plus the 30 taken out of jail, let's call this 1000 Tories) 500 in front, 200 in the middle, 500 in the back, the line of men would stretch 3,600 feet in length, that's almost ¾ of a mile long (.63 to be exact). The map below shows, to scale, the assumed position and length, labeled as "S" and "P" for soldier and prisoner, as to their location, and more importantly, their length along the road. This played a significant role in the battle as the long column of men were meandering down the rolling hills of the Lindley Mill area, and then fording Cane Creek. A ford was well known as a strategic location, since it represents a bottle-neck. This impedes the speed of movement, and seriously limits the ability to take alternative routes (scatter).

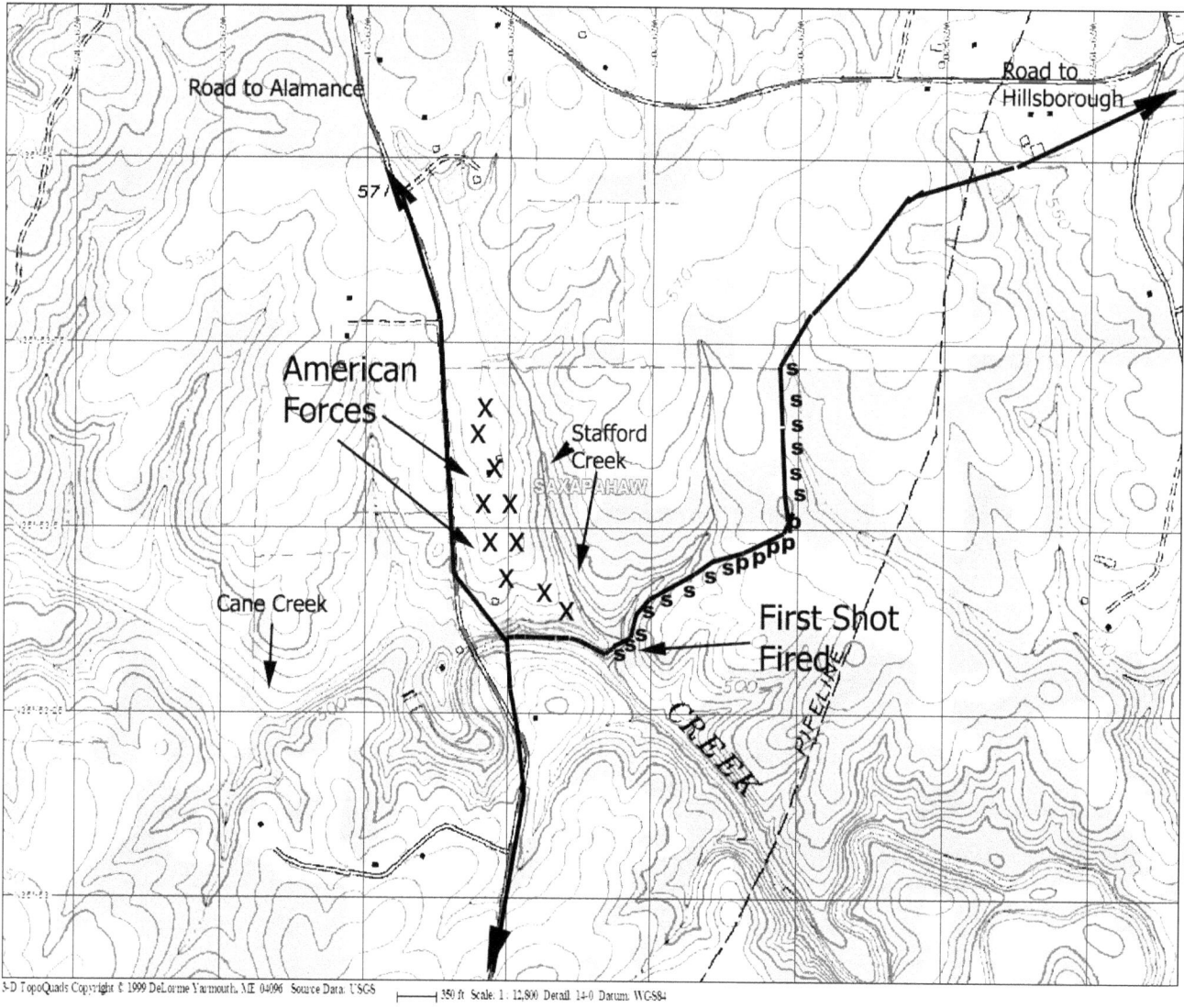

General Butler and his men selected their attack wisely. The ambush was set at an interesting location, geographically. The combination of hilly terrain, a tight bend in the roadway, Cane Creek needing to be forded, brought about a properly established plan. However, as stated earlier, it was a little more difficult to "attack" Fanning's men since they were spread out over a long distance, coupled with having Patriot prisoners amongst them (collateral damage). There is an assumption that Fanning's men became aware of the Americans location, maybe by a noise made, or someone being seen etc. David Fanning seemed to imply they were not properly "on guard" to the precipitous location. David Fanning states, *"Col'n McNeal, who had the advance guard, had neglected to take the necessary precautions for our safety, and by information of Capt. McLain, Cumberland County, Little River; and as soon as I had discovered the situation, we were in, and having so great a number of prisoners, I left my station, and pushed for the advance guard; on my coming up with Col'n McNeal, I inquired the reason of his neglect; and before he could answer, we were fired upon by the rebels. They killed eight men, among them was Col'n McNeal, who received three balls through him and five through his horse."* If they had not fired so early, and the soldiers were fording Cane Creek, the prisoners would have been near Stafford's Branch and maybe they would have won the battle. Then again, maybe the prisoners would have suffered casualties, since they would have been in-between both enemy and friendly fire, not a great circumstance.

(Here is a picture of the actual road bed, just before crossing the ford at Stafford Creek)

This image shows the battle site from the Tories view, heading towards Cane Creek. In fact, it is hidden from view, due to the slopping land. The arrow shows the approximate location of the ambush, illustrating the rolling terrain.

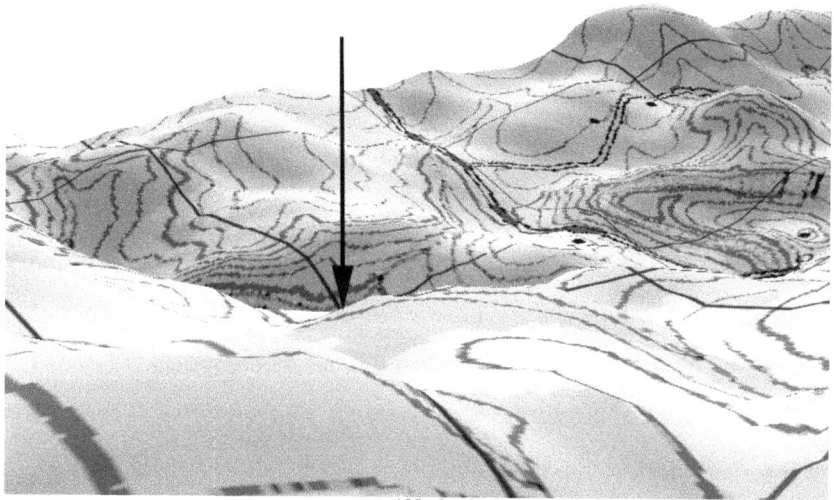

First shot was fired as the leading Tories crossed Stafford Creek, where the road turns west towards the ford on Cane Creek. Because of this attack at the "head" of the line, as opposed to letting the Tories pass further (allowing them to be more exposed to fire), it is assumed the Tories knew they were in a trap. Despite what occurred (some speculate it was a noise or maybe the cocking of a rifle etc.), the battle began, and further back ¼ mile were the prisoners. It is assumed they moved the prisoners to either a barn or the Spring Meeting House. Since the Spring Meeting House was about a mile away, it is believed they were stashed into a local barn. Local tradition states an old barn foundation was known to be in the general area of the battle site. Regardless, with the prisoners out of the way, and under guard, the Tories were able to fully engage the Patriot militia.

(Here is a picture of the exact location of the first shot fired, the road bed is on the right and Stafford's creek is on the left. Stories mention that this creek shown here, flowed red, due to the dead and wounded.)

With all the Tories behind Col. McNeal, (now dead along with six other Tories), they regrouped, and Fanning describes this, "*I then ordered a retreat back to where we left the prisoners and after securing them, I made the necessary preparations to attack the enemy..*" The American forces were on the west side of Stafford

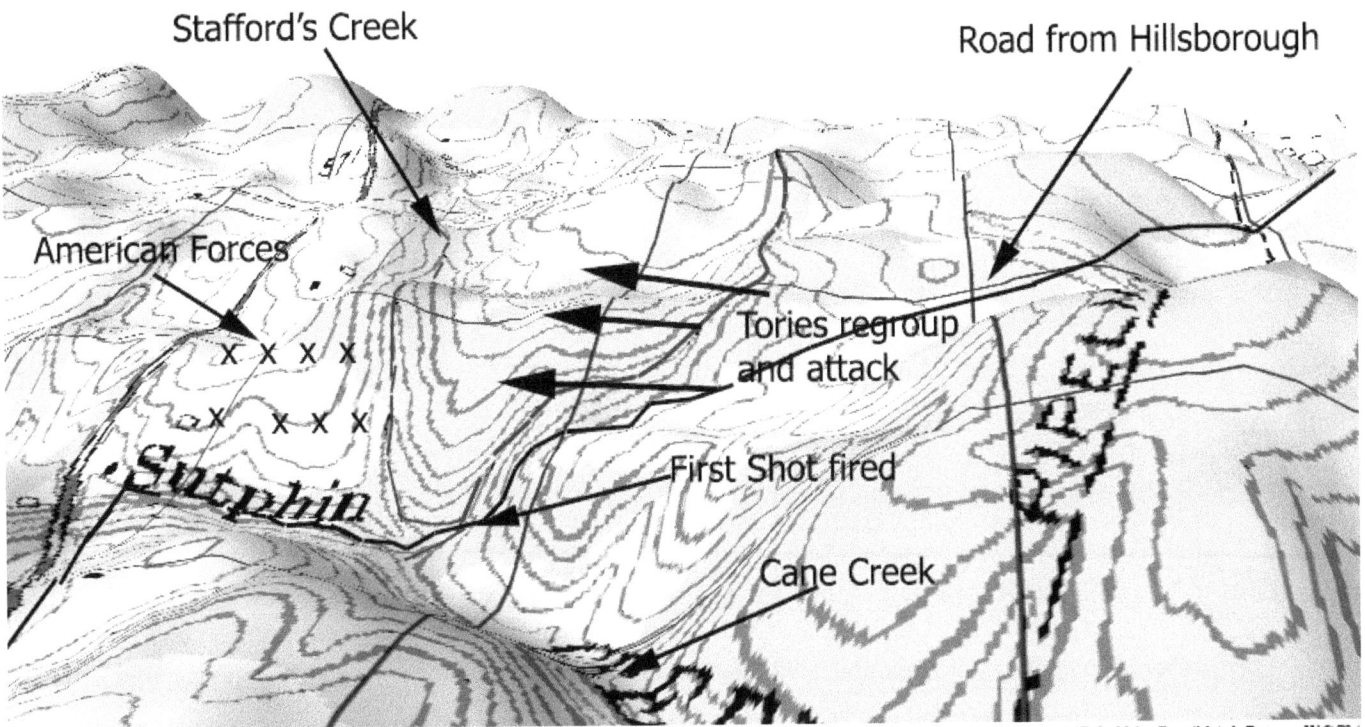

Creek, and this elevated location required the Tories to cross two creeks, thus having to work their way up the hilly terrain, under fire. As you can see in the above map, two creeks join together right by the roadbed, where it fords them. Below is a panorama picture of the location where the two creeks meet, Stafford on the left and the unnamed creek on the right. This picture is taken exactly at the ford, where the road crosses these "joined creeks".

Here is a picture of the "American Forces" location on a knoll as shown on the map from the prior page (white area of the USGS map).

Another interesting discussion about this battle, which wasn't found in most Revolutionary conflicts, was the battles duration, documented to be four hours (most battles considered lengthy were one hour in length). For example, one large conflict in the Revolutionary War, was the battle at King's Mountain. There, 1,200 Patriots fought 1,500 British troops, for one hour, defeating the entire British force, many were killed and the remaining captured. Here at Lindley Mill, the conflict ended due to both sides running out of ammunition. In one pension it stated they had – "*11 fires*" before running out of ammunition. How long does a battle take with 11 rounds of ammunition? In other pension applications they document the battle with varying durations (1 hour, 2 hours, and 3-4 hours). It is probable the four hour duration was arrival to departure, and during this total duration, there were *significant lulls*. It was *not* four hours of *continual shooting*.

Here is a possible scenario of how the four hours transpired:

- First fire, where Patriot forces surprised the Tories.

- The Tories (which were spread out in a long line) regrouped.

- Guards had to be established (separate from those men to fight) to control the prisoners.

- A battle strategy established, and men put into position.

- Fanning then starts his offensive maneuvers and catches the Patriots by surprise, whilst they were waiting and trying to figure out what was going on (during the lull).

All of that effort – took time. In most pensions, it states the attack by the Tories, was a surprise. It was this "surprise" attack when most Patriots were wounded or killed. What was this duration between first fire and the Tories surprise attack? Why were the Patriots caught off guard or surprised? *Probably due to the lull when the Tories were regrouping.*

Finally the American forces retreated, and Fanning threatened to have the prisoners killed if the Americans attempted to free them. Fanning stated, "*…and after engaging them four hours they retreated. I lost twenty-seven men killed, and sixty so badly wounded, that they could not be moved ; besides thirty slightly, but so that they could keep up with the main body.*" One pension documents this threat (William C. Smith) he writes, "*…met the enemy and changed a few rounds of fire. When they presently retreated they sent word if we pursued them they would put to death the American prisoners they had taken…Col Mabane thought most expedient not to pursue them immediately so we remained there a short time in order to learn the maneuvers and to ascertain which way they were aiming…*"

Here is a picture of the original road, on your right is the Stafford Creek ford, where the men had to make a tight, almost "U" turn around the knoll, and head west towards the Cane Creek ford (near the mill site).

Fanning was mortally wounded, and he states, "*At the conclusion of this action, I received a shot in my left arm, which broke the bone in several pieces ; my lost blood was so great, that I was taken off my horse, and led to a secret place in the woods.*" It is amazing American forces did not scour the woods. Maybe the issue of not having any more ammunition, prevented staying around. Fanning continued, "*I also desired that Major Rains return as soon as he could leave Col. McDugald ; as I thought he might be the means of saving me from the hands of the enemies. At the departure of the my little army, I was left with three men and in four days 17 more came to my assistance.*" He also learned later, more about the battle as he commented, "*The party we had engaged I found consisted of four hundred Continentals under the command of Col'o Maybin [Mebane] and Gen'l Butler. In twenty-four days I found myself able to set up and then dispatched four of my Captains…*" It is assumed that David Fanning was under the care of a local Doctor and Loyalist – Dr. John Pyle. Dr. Pyle lived less than a mile from the battle site (more about Fanning's wounds later on).

Rev. E.E. Caruthers wrote about this battle in his book (The Old North State), from actual interviews with decedents in the 1850's. Caruthers documents that Col. Robert Mebane was a hero in the Patriot's line, as his commanding officer Gen Butler ordered a retreat (like at Camden and later on) and Col Mebane rallied the troops to continue fighting. Mebane later presented his sword to the General due to his disobeying orders, but the General refused. Also documented by Caruthers, was the story in which Col Mebane was distributing gun powder to the men (via his hat), as ammunition was depleting.

The battle ended, leaving the wounded and dead in the field, creek, and elsewhere. Some residents came to doctor the remaining men. Some wives (tradition or stories) traveled many miles to take care of their men, while others came to comfort the severely wounded until they died. Tradition also states, that a mass grave was dug where 34 men were buried, and a depression was visible at the edge of the field, near a spring. Visiting this precise location, no depression could be recognized, amongst the forested landscape. The spring was still flowing, and a very old spring box remained in rather good condition. The spring is shown above and the "edge of the field, is pictured to the right.

As with all battles, the (dead/wounded) count varies. Less information that is documented *immediately* following the battle, more variance tends to occur. Below is a table (NA=not mentioned or available) that gathers all the accounts (from pensions and books) that provide any details. Not everyone was dead at the battle site. Typically there would be more wounded than dead. One pensioner said he was left for dead, but was nursed back to health (13 pieces of skull bone missing) and survived!

Pension	Fanning	Caruthers	S3011	S9410	R1185	S4421	R7071	R3635	S2841
Patriot wounded	90	50	NA	NA	NA	NA	himself	3	7
Patriot dead	24	16	50	17	A good many	several	4	4	5
Tory wounded	60		NA	NA	NA				
Tory dead	27		15	100	A good many	30-40	37 + 26	36	several
Patriot count	400	300	4-500	250	4-500	NA	NA	200	NA
Tory count	705	600	6-800	700	900	NA	NA		NA

There are numerous stories about the disposition of the dead. Some say they were buried in a mass grave, others infer they were buried at the Quaker (Spring Meeting House) cemetery, and others relate they were taken home and buried there. One pension (S3011) stated, *"In counting the dead we found we had lost fifty and had killed fifteen Tories we buried the dead on the creek side, putting all the Tories into one pit and marched back to the barracks …."* Caruthers said the neighbors came and took care of the wounded, and buried 32 in one pit. Caruthers also states, *"A friend, in writing to me from the Scotch region, says, that 'including all of both side who were slain on the field, and all who died soon after in consequence of their wounds, the number could not be much under a hundred; and this estimate, which looks quite reasonable, taking everything into view, we suppose to be not far from the truth."* Several pensions state "a few", "some", and "a good many" as to the wounded and dead (now combining these two categories).

Who fought for the patriots, and who were their commanders? Here is the question that will never be fully known. Following is a table from 6,600 "southern campaign" pensions that were sorted, in order to locate specific pensions dealing with Lindley Mill. What is well known are the commanders, especially Butler, Mebane, Luttrell, and Nalls. The difficulty lies in the identification of the common militia man. However, generally speaking, this battle was documented more thoroughly (pension records), than most battles in North Carolina (except Guilford Courthouse).

In the Public Record Office in England (PRO), there were letters filed by loyalists claiming "half-pay", and other issues (primarily lost land from the confiscation acts). In one record, a Loyalist who served with Fanning provided details about the situation (never published before). Kenneth Stewart of the North Carolina Highland Regiment provides this account (PRO X/J 6304) – April 4, 1786, *"…That your memorialist in the year 1776 in conformity to Governor Martin's instructions did take arms in support of his Majesty's Government and continued his exertions, until he was made prisoner of war at Moor's Creek Bridge – That your memorialist soon after made his escape from the enemy and joined the British Troops on their landing in Georgia…That your memorialist in the year 1781 was stationed in Wilmington in North Carolina under the command of Colonel Craig [actually Major] when he was ordered to march with part of his Corps, joined some of the Loyal Militia to Hillsborough where lay a body of the enemy under the command of the Rebel Governor – that the loyal part on this occasion made upwards of one hundred and fifty prisoners that on conveying them to the Garrison at Wilmington, there was an attempt made by a party of the Rebels who concentrated themselves at a pass near Lindley's Mill to risk them friends – at this place a hot action commenced when the Highlanders, after sustaining some loss drove the enemy and returned all the prisoners they had taken – that your memorialist in this last action, had a bullet shot through his body and as the wound was immediately considered mortal he was left as irrecoverably on the field – that your memorialist in this situation was near a year before he recovered sufficient strength to walk, nor have it in his power to convey intelligence to his friends, of hit being alive which circumstances has been the cause of his not being returned to half pay, along with the other officers of his corps – That your memorialist as soon as he was able, made shift to get to Nova Scotia where he has lived ever since on the bounty of his friend Lieu Colonel Stewart with whom he is retuned within these few days to England…"* The interesting part of this account was another confirmation of the captured being 150 men.

Here is a table of those pension transcribed by the wonderful effort of the Southern Campaign (www.southerncampaign.org/pen - which at this time of writing – August 2009 - has transcribed 6619 pensions.)

Albright	Ludwick	Lindley Mill	Col Mebane
Allison	James	Lindley Mill	Col Mebane, volunteered Capt. Thompson "light horse" for Orange County
Allman	Nathan	Lindley Mill	Served under Luttrell (fought to free brother)
Blalock	David	Lindley Mill	Gen Butler, Col Nalls, Col Littrell, Lieu Rob Jones
Bledsoe	Lewis	Lindley Mill	fought at Lindley's Mill - held our ground - returned to Hillsborough
Brener	Isaac	Lindley Mill	Capt. William Smith, John Nalls, Robert Mebane, provided details of battle
Brewer	Isaac	Lindley Mill	Supposed to be 900 Tories, we supposed to have 4-500 lasted 1 hour, Brewer wounded
Brownlow	John	Lindley Mill	Capt Joseph Russer, Col Mebane, wounded left for dead 13-pieces of skull bone
Clark	James	Lindley Mill	fought with Col Mebane and Gen Butler - said 77 horses strong
Collins	Eli	Lindley Mill	Attached Fanning at Lindley's Mill
Copeland	John	Lindley Mill	Served under Nells - said 14 died
Draffon	John	Lindley Mill	Capt Cage at Luttrells Barracks, fought at Lindley's Mill
Earthman	Isaac	Lindley Mill	Capt Gwinn, sent to watch the Tories leaving Hillsboro, fought at Lindley - Fanning killed
Edwards	Robert	Lindley Mill	Under Gen Butler and Col Mebane, doesn't remember his Capt.
Elkins	Joshua	Lindley Mill	Under Capt McCullers
Fooshee	Elijah	Lindley Mill	we had 80, commenced at 9am, Capt Duck killed, continued about 1 hour
Forrest	James	Lindley Mill	two parties fought at Lindleys, Whigs were overpowered compelled to retreat
Geane	Phillip	Lindley Mill	Pension states that he was one of those **killed at the battle**
Greeen	William	Lindley Mill	counted 31 dead on the ground besides others near the mill, Luttrell died later
Gregory	William	Lindley Mill	joined Capt Alexander Clark, joined Ben Gbutlers met Tories at Lindley's Mill
Grist	Benjamin	Lindley Mill	Capt. Clendennen & Col Belford - he was wounded in the head at the battle Lindley Mill
Higdon	Daniel	Lindley Mill	said he knew that his friend Billy Dillard was killed
Howell	Benjamin	Lindley Mill	Col Luttrell and Maj Nalls killed - we whipped them, drove them to Raft Swamp
Ivy	Henry	Lindley Mill	fought at Lindley Mill with a part of toried under Col Fanning.
Johnson	Robert	Lindley Mill	killed 36 Tories
Kell	James	Lindley Mill	Col Mebane
Manis	Seth	Lindley Mill	sharp action, he retreated and we dod not take him nor any of his men
Marler	Joseph	Lindley Mill	had a skirmish with the Tories near a place called Lindley's Mill in which Tories defeated
McDavis	Massey	Lindley Mill	Gen Butler, Capt Clark - he gave details of battle
McElroy	John	Lindley Mill	Capt. Lewis Bledsoe originally under Capt. McCuller's Company
McElroy	Micajah	Lindley Mill	Col Mebane in charge, fought tories
Meachem	Richard	Lindley Mill	9 miles from Luttrell's, I was wounded in the hip, 37 scotts and 26 tories, 4 patriots killed
Meares	Joel	Lindley Mill	Marched against Fanning and McNeil who commanded 700 Tories
Miles	Thomas	Lindley Mill	Capt Foley and his 48 volunteers from Chatham Co. some details given
Mitchell	William	Lindley Mill	Col Maben, were some 30 or 40 tories killed and several of our little force
Mitchell	Jesse	Lindley Mill	Lieu Abraham Bryant, Jacob Duck, Robert Maybin, skirmish at Lindley's Mill
Moore	Henry	Lindley Mill	under Capt McFarland, 5 men were killed, Col Luttrell and 7 wounded, killed several Tory
Moore	James	Lindley Mill	McDouglad (tory) killed, Nalls killed - there were 250 prisoners from Hillsboro
Myrick	Moses	Lindley Mill	Under Capt. Jacob Duck, rendezvoused at Maj Nall residence, then fought at Lindley
Neely	Joseph	Lindley Mill	Capt Nells, Col Mebane - gave details
Nichols	William	Lindley Mill	he said they won, took prisoners! Said they fought along the side of a long hill
Parrish	Claiborne	Lindley Mill	Party of tories took prisoners-we intercepted at Lindley's Mill where we had engagement
Pearson	Paris	Lindley Mill	application filed by his wife, said he was in a horse company under Butler
Poplin	George	Lindley Mill	Under Maj Nalls, battle lasted 3 hours, Col Goldston, Mebane in command
Ragains	Thomas	Lindley Mill	routed them, took 25 prisoners to Mr. Lindley's house
Ray	William	Lindley Mill	Captain of Orange Co. Militia under Mebane and Butler, fought at Lindley's Mill
Smith	Buckner	Lindley Mill	Capt. Clendennen under Col Lytle fought at Lindley's Mill, 4 wounds, scars remain
Smith	William	Lindley Mill	Changed a few rounds, told they would kill prisoners, we waited to see where they went
Standifer	Benjamin	Lindley Mill	he knew that Luttrell and Nells died
Stroud	Matthew	Lindley Mill	difficult to read - Mentions Nells and Butler
Williams	David	Lindley Mill	under Col Taylor, 200 Patriots, 30-40 Tory killed, Tories had 406 men
Wood	John	Lindley Mill	took most of the citizens of Orange County prisoner, fought at Lindley's Mill

Jesse Benton also provided information about the battle. Remember he stated – *"we dispatched three men to find Genl Butler which they effected a little before day & gave him the first account of what has happened.*) Then the letter continues, *"He then threw himself in the Enemys Road below Doctor Pile's & marched up to Lindley's Mill where he met the Tories, engaged them immediately & gave them a total defeat, tho the prisoners were carried off by them. Upwards of fifty Tories killed; Col Litterell [Lutteral], Maj. Nalls & six privates on our side killed. Col Hector McNeil, Capt Doud, one M. Cloud & several men in officers garb among the Tories were left dead. The Highlanders ventured with only Broadsword & Dirks so near that they received both powder & ball at the same time & fell like heroes indeed."* It seems that everyone is in agreement with the officer death toll, but as to the common man, it's not well documented. It is also worth noting (according to Benton) that three men were sent to tell Butler, and then Butler went to battle. (Note: this document differs with the traditional local story - as to how Butler was notified - that Alexander Mebane escaped through the tall grass, thus alerting Butler.)

In the continuation of the letter from James Iredell, written (Sept.16, 1781) just after the attack on Hillsborough, he writes, *"On Wednesday morning last, about 7 o'clock, a large body of Tories, supposed to amount to 400, under Fanning and McNeil, entered Hillsborough, and with very little loss from the fire of an inconsiderable guard, got possession of the Governor, Col. Read, Mr. Huske, Col. Lyttle, and a number of other persons. Lyttle, though a prisoner on parole, was hacked and cut by Fanning in a most cruel manner. The persons of the others do not appear to have been ill-used. They continued in town till two, rifling and plundering, and doing a good deal of mischief, and then carried off their prisoners and booty, making even the Governor walk on foot. During the time they were in town, they released the prisoners that were in goal [jail], put arms in their hands, and turned the guard into their places. Some were killed in attempting to make their escape, and it is said three of four of the Tories were killed by the guards' fire. Two of the men at first came to Mr. Hogg's house, and insulted and abused him a good deal, and robbed him of his watch and buckles, and made him deliver up his keys but he afterwards obtained a sentinel to be placed at his house, and he suffered on the whole little other loss than that of his watch. We have since had an imperfect account of the rear guard of these rascals being attacked and routed with great loss by about 150 men under Col. Mebane (a most spirited continental officer). The Tories were far more numerous, but they nevertheless lost most of their horses, guns, and the plunder they brought from Hillsborough. Seven of our men were killed, the number of wounded uncertain, but among these Col. Lutrell was shot through the body, though it is thought he may recover. The rest of the Tories (supposed to amount to about 200) were with the prisoners two miles in front. Every effort was making to bring on a successful attack, and God grant such a one may have taken place! The action was near Deep River, about forty miles from Hillsborough, a little above Ramsay's Mills."* This is an amazing letter, in that, it was written so soon after the event, with such differing views of what occurred. Is this the truth, since it was written so early? Or was this another example of the story being altered as it was passed to him (since Iredell was not captured)?

Fanning sent his men, along with the prisoners, to Wilmington transferring the prisoners to British authorities. Caruthers states *"From Cane Creek, they went directly to their head-quarters on the Raft Swamp, and after crossing Deep river they stayed all night at the house of Mr. McRae, father of the present Collin McRae, Esq."* This is the only documented stop or camp, although you can be certain they rested many times, along the way. Caruthers continues the story at this location, *"The Governor was put into an additional apartment, at the end of the house, and there closely quartered."* And it continues, *"By way of retaliation, my mother made some attempts before the day to let her namesake, the Governor, escape, but without success."* Her mother's maiden name was Burke, although not a direct relative. Caruthers' story ends, *"The Governor appears to have been treated with as much courtesy, and to have had his situation made as comfortable on the road, as could be expected."*

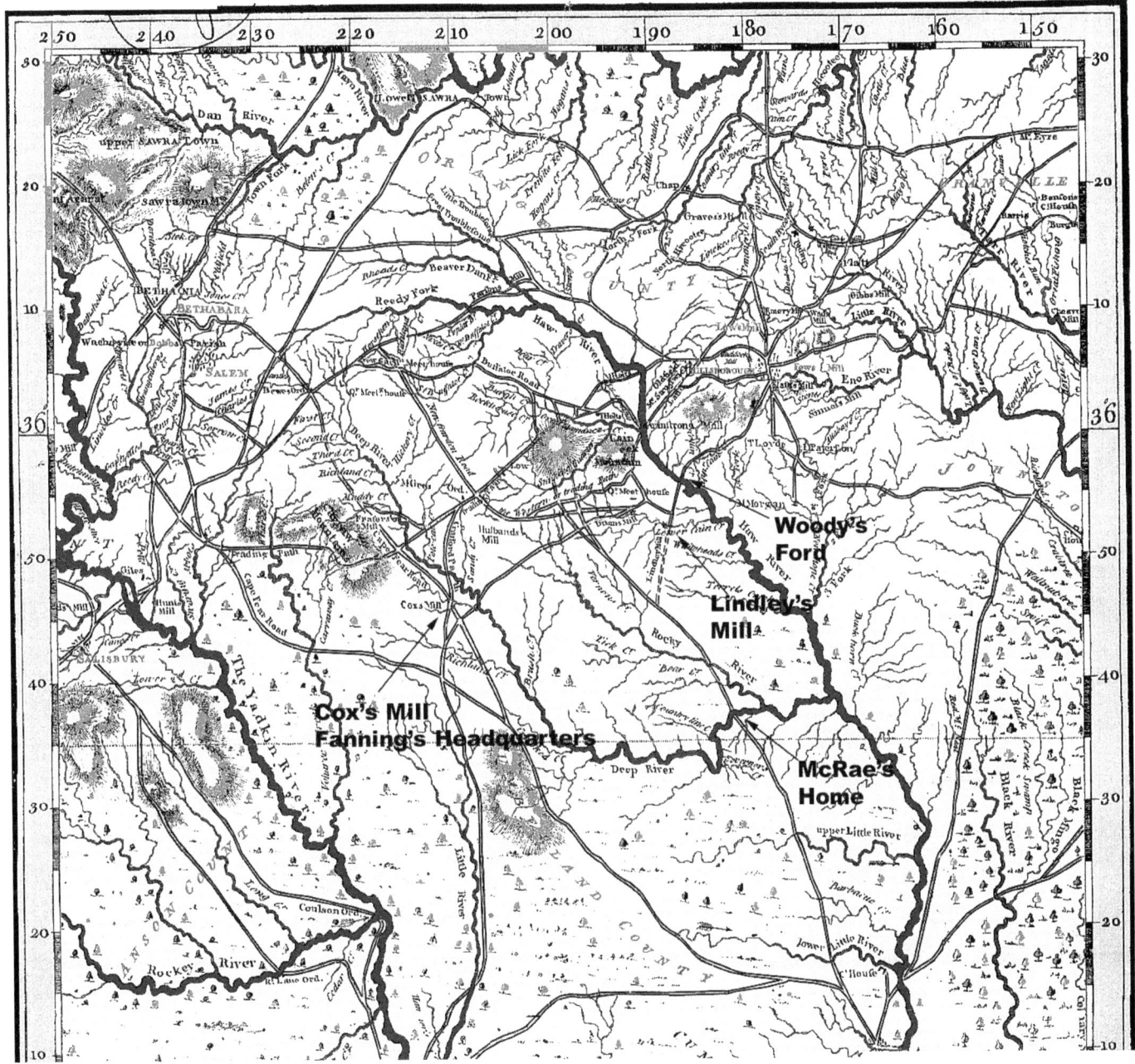

In a letter from Archibald Maclaine to James Iredell September 21, 1781 he gives this account, *"….but the intelligence which we have received of the Governor being taken at Hillsborough, may give a fatal turn to our affairs; as this is not the 10th day since it happened, you may probably have heard of it. The town of Hillsborough was plundered, and the Tories retreated with the Governor, and it is said about 100 Continental soldiers, and several officers, to some place near Lindley's Mill The paroled officers were taken, and Col. Lyttle much wounded, though he was unarmed. Whilst their horses were tied in a thicket, and their plunder displayed in an old field, two of the opposite parties met and engaged, which occasioned a smart action of the whole under Butler and Mabin, and though we wanted ammunition, they kept the field with clubbed muskets. The Tories fled, leaving their horses and plunder, but in the beginning of the action had sent off their prisoners under a guard through Guilford. McNeil killed and Fanning's left arm broken. Many of these particulars are from Absalom Tatum, who had been taken, and escaped in a dark night, and was got to Mr. Rand's. The prisoners are pursued by 200 of our horse, and expresses sent to waylay the passes; but Brown of Bladen has few men, and the Tories about him are numerous."* (See *Life and Correspondence of James Iredell Vol 1* pg. 549-550) Absalom Tatum was a respectable attorney in Hillsborough, and you would assume from a first hand account his story would be accurate (although being re-told by Maclaine). This is the only account stating that prisoners were sent away, therefore, the battle would not have freed them at all. This account is plausible, but probably didn't occur, due to the large quantity of Tories required to guard the prisoners (in a march formation). In a building, the prisoners would have been confined (i.e. in a barn), and easier to control (shoot someone leaving a door or window), requiring less men to guard, and more men available to fight. Therefore it would appear that this account was not accurate.

David Fanning (severely wounded) was left behind, supposedly hidden in the woods, so the Patriots could not find him. Stories include he was hidden in a cave, where he was cared for. Initially, it would seem rational to be hidden in the woods. However, since Doctor John Pyle was just south of the battle site (less than a mile), he was certainly involved in Fanning's care or in hiding him. Dr. John Pyle is a well known loyalist doctor. In a letter from William O'Neal (written to Gov. Burke) he stated that Dr. Pyle had been involved in caring for wounded patriots at Lindley's Mill, (March 19, 1782) *"…We at the time had several men wounded. I ordered him to take charge of the wounded, which he did, and proved very faithful…"* However, it is certain he was also doctoring Fanning. This could have been the cloak. Why would Dr. Pyle be searched (for Fanning), while caring for the patriots? Unfortunately, nothing documents Fanning's movements after receiving his wound, from either his letters to Major Craig, or his diary.

In a letter from British Craig to David Fanning he writes, (PRO) October 13, 1781, *"…I have been unfortunate enough to have the list of medicines you sent me, however I will desire the surgeons to send you such as he thinks most likely to be serviceable – tho from his not being acquainted with your case it is all by guess, I am much concerned to find the probability of so may of your people suffering from want of necessary and attendance – nothing shall be wanted in my power either in that respect or in that of salt for their relief. I am not at liberty to explain myself in a letter but I hope I shall very soon have it in my power to assist them with greater ease than at present..."* Dr. Pyle may have required specific medicines that he was unable to acquire, or would have raised suspicion, so Fanning sends a list to Craig. In this same letter, Craig discusses (what is assumed) Fanning's horse (or one of his dead officers), *"...The circumstance of the circumstances of the Stallion you mention, I determined it in your favor and took him away from Mr. Campbell, or rather, from a gentleman to whom he sold him, he has been with my horses ever since and never rode, I now send him to you by Captain Linley – The long northerly wind, have prevented any arrival from Charles Town so that we are totally without news. I wish I had got Mr. Burkes papers. J. Craig."* Obviously Capt. Lindley knew where Fanning was "hidden", and who was doctoring him.

The Second Attempt – Brown Marsh and Livingston's Bridge

This part of the ordeal is not that well documented, if at all. There was a concerted effort to try and catch the Tories, and free the prisoners – two more times. Fortunately, British Maj. Craig writes about this situation, and provides the reader with the British account. Pension records highlight some detail, but varies in specifics, from record to record.

Most pension document a group Patriot militia men were rounded up, mainly in the Chatham County area, under the command of Col. William Moore, and then rendezvous with Gen Butler and Col Mebane. It should be noted that Gov Burke never writes about these subsequent battles in order to free him. Burke wrote many letters, none however, discussed these final attempts to free him.

There are conflicting stories (as usual) in the pension records. Some records mention Brown Marsh as the first and only battle, others mention Brown and Livingston Creek (or bridge). As you might expect, some pensions discuss these two battles in opposite order (which occurred first). Finally, the British account was written soon after the event, therefore the *sequence of events* should be rather accurate.

Location – Brown Marsh

Where is this battle site? It is on the road from Cross Creek (Fayetteville) to Wilmington. As with most 18th century locations, the precise spot is rather difficult to ascertain, especially with varying locations being reported. First, some ambiguities need clarification (if possible). Brown Creek intersects the Cape Fear River near Elizabethtown (shown in the map below). This river originates from the headwaters, of Brown Swamp (or marsh). The swamp (or marsh) is located about two miles south of Elizabethtown (this map is shown on the next page). Lastly, some pensions document Brown Ferry, which is on the Cape Fear River and not associated with the Brown River or Brown Mash.

Precisely where the battle occurred is undetermined. However, it could be at either a road/bridge location, a road crossing Brown Creek, or further south on the road crossing Brown Marsh.

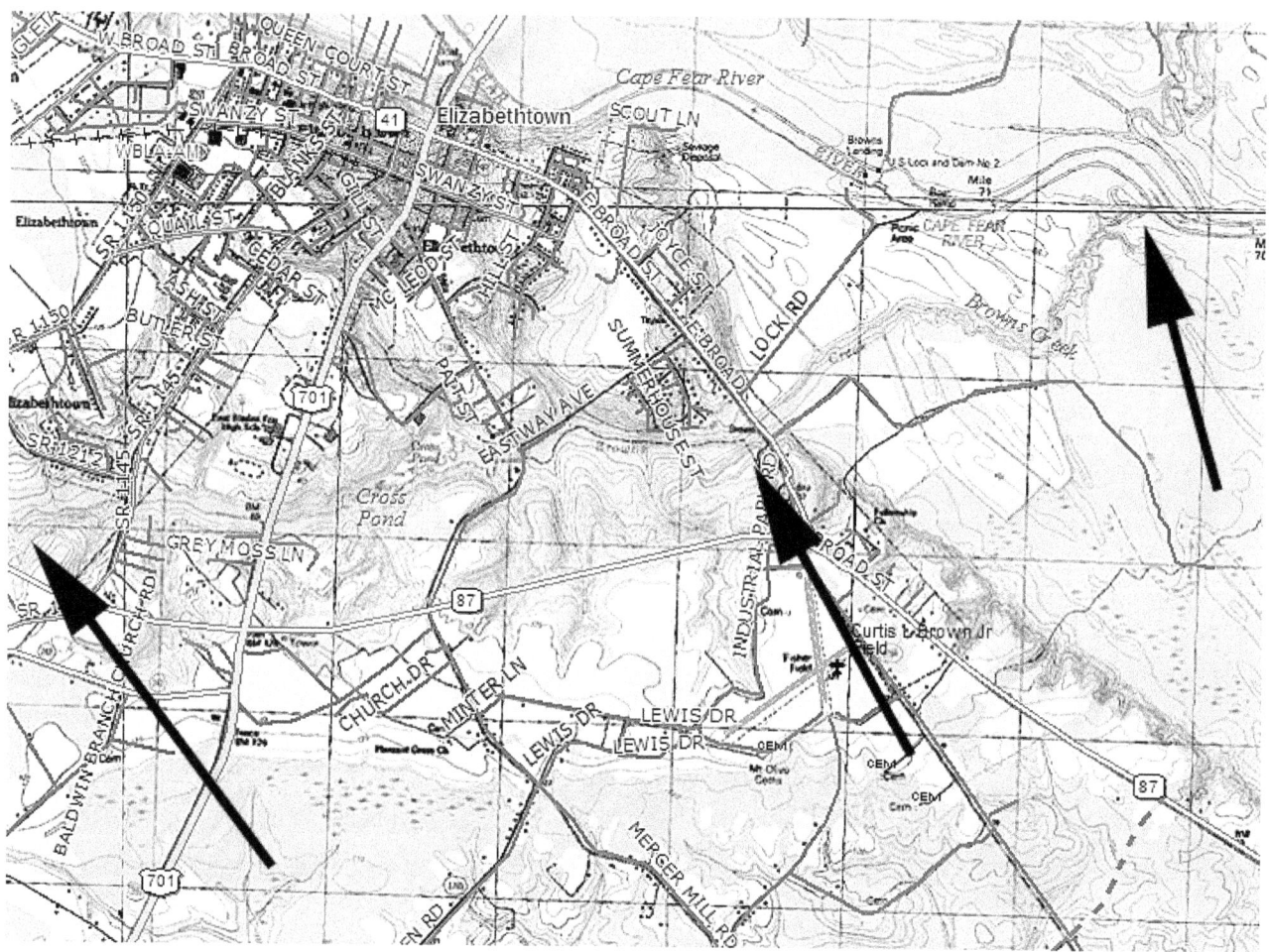

In Craig's letter dated October 22, 1781 (N.C. Archives, British Records, 1781 – X/L05252) he writes describing Fanning's two key officers, *"...Col Ray who met them at Raft Swamp and Col McDougal who jointly managed rather than commanded them from thence have also very great merit, the later distinguished himself much in the action with Butler – the route they came from Hillsborough here is upwards of two hundred and thirty miles through a country which it is nare possible to have an idea of without seeing it- their difficulties from every circumstance of want of provisions, fatigue and the danger of being intercepted were such as required great resolution to content with and at last they would have failed in their hopes of reaching this had we not marched out to support them which was without any previous communications with them and I only guessed at their route from my knowledge of their usual method of conducting themselves."* It is interesting to note that in this part of his description, he alludes to an engagement at the "Raft Swamp". His letter continues, *"Gen Butler having mounted between four and five hundred men marched so rapidly to get possession of the pass at Livingston Creek that he reached it within three or four hours after they had joined me – indeed his march was so rapid that I could not conceive it to be him and I must candidly confess that error, prevented our destroying his corps completely for he as little expected to see us as I did him of the appearance of forty or fifty of his horse. I took it for a Col Brown who I knew to have about that number and ordered the cavalry supported by about 60 infantry to push them which they did for two or three miles and fell in with about two hundred more who were very advantageously posted there they drove also but then returned in consequence of my orders even tho it might perhaps not have*

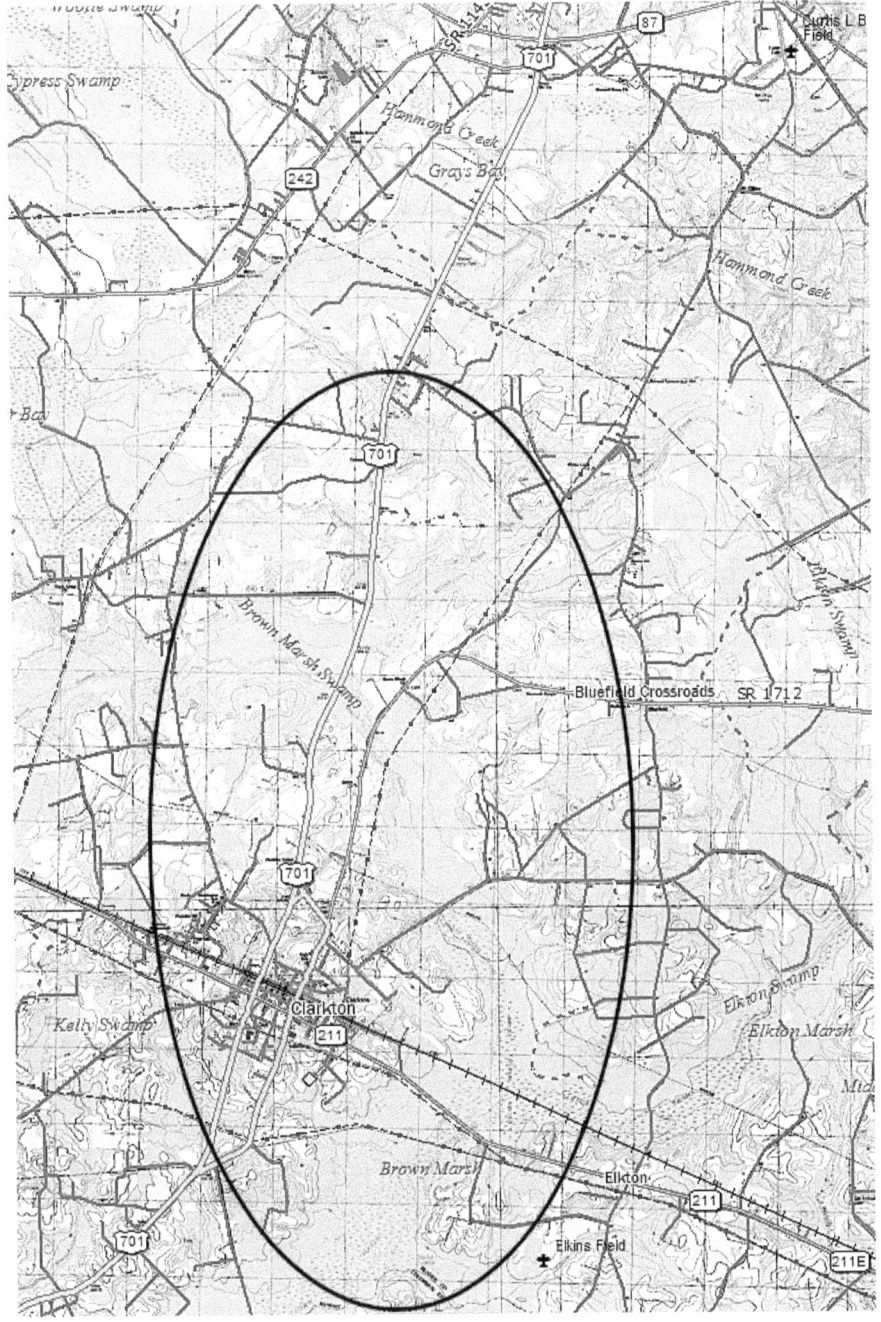

been too late could not have marched the distance in the time we had one man of my troops wounded." Now we have an engagement at Livingston Creek, or the bridge across it. This area is very near Wilmington (approximately 16 miles). From the patriot pensions more information can be determined. William Mitchell (S4221) states, *"...Butler then turned our course immediately down the Cape Fear River for Wilmington to Brown's Ferry on Cape Fear River where we crossed over and there encamped for two or three days. We received reinforcements of Col. William Moore's Regiment yet it did not join him until we crossed the river at Brown's Ferry. Here Butler broke up his camp believing himself strong enough to cope with Fanning and set out on a forced march to overtake him although Fanning had received reinforcement of about 300 British soldiers under the command of Major Craig. We overtook him at Livingston's Swamp. This declarant's brother Lieu. David Mitchell was officer of the day. The action was brought on under very auspicious circumstance but Butler took another panic supposing Fanning to have artillery crossed out <u>'Soldiers retreat they have cannon and we cannot stand them'</u> and he, Taylor and Moore ran off with all who pursue their flight and but for the bravery and disinterested services of Co. Robert Mebane of whom this declarant already spoke the whole army would have been probably cut to pieces at the swamp. But he rallied one hundred and fifty or two hundred of the troops and put them in order of battle and resisted the pursuit of Fanning who finding that a sharp conflict had again ensued supposed that Butler's whole force had fallen back to that point intentionally and they he was induced to fall back in his turn as night closed the scene...."* This pension statement, "set out on a forced march to overtake him", corroborates Craig's description – of their rapid march.

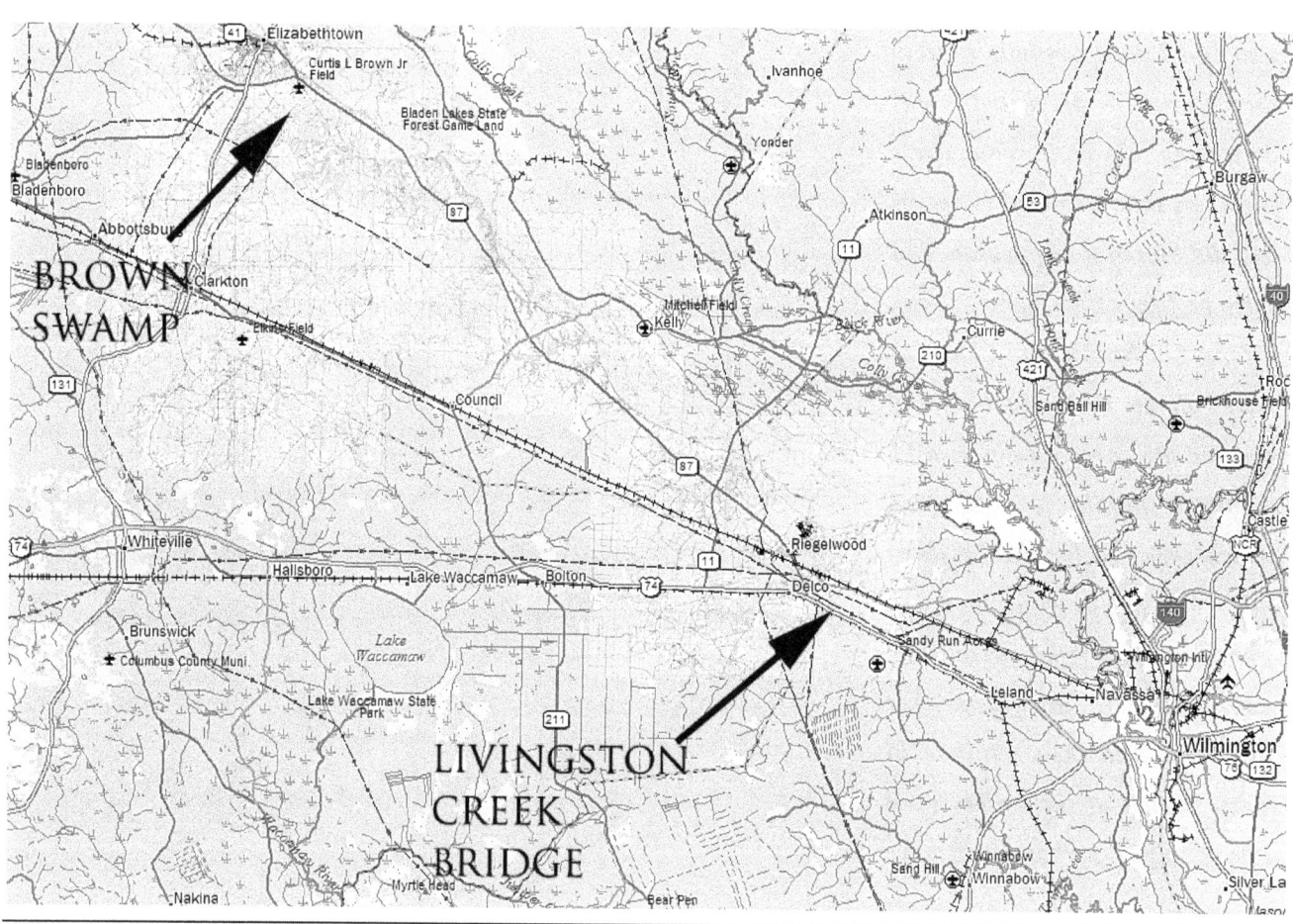

More pensions support the situation at Livingston's Bridge. In another pension, Robert Browning supported the retreat story (Butler), ***"...They continued their march under General Butler's company until the enemy viz. the Tories were overtaken near the town of Wilmington – so soon as General Butler with his forces overtook the enemy...he (general Butler) ordered his Army to put themselves in battle array, which was done accordingly: no sooner however was the Army arrayed for battle, then Gen Butler ordered a retreat, assigning as his only reason for such a course as this, that the Tories had artillery and he had none. General Butler retreated back for several miles.."***

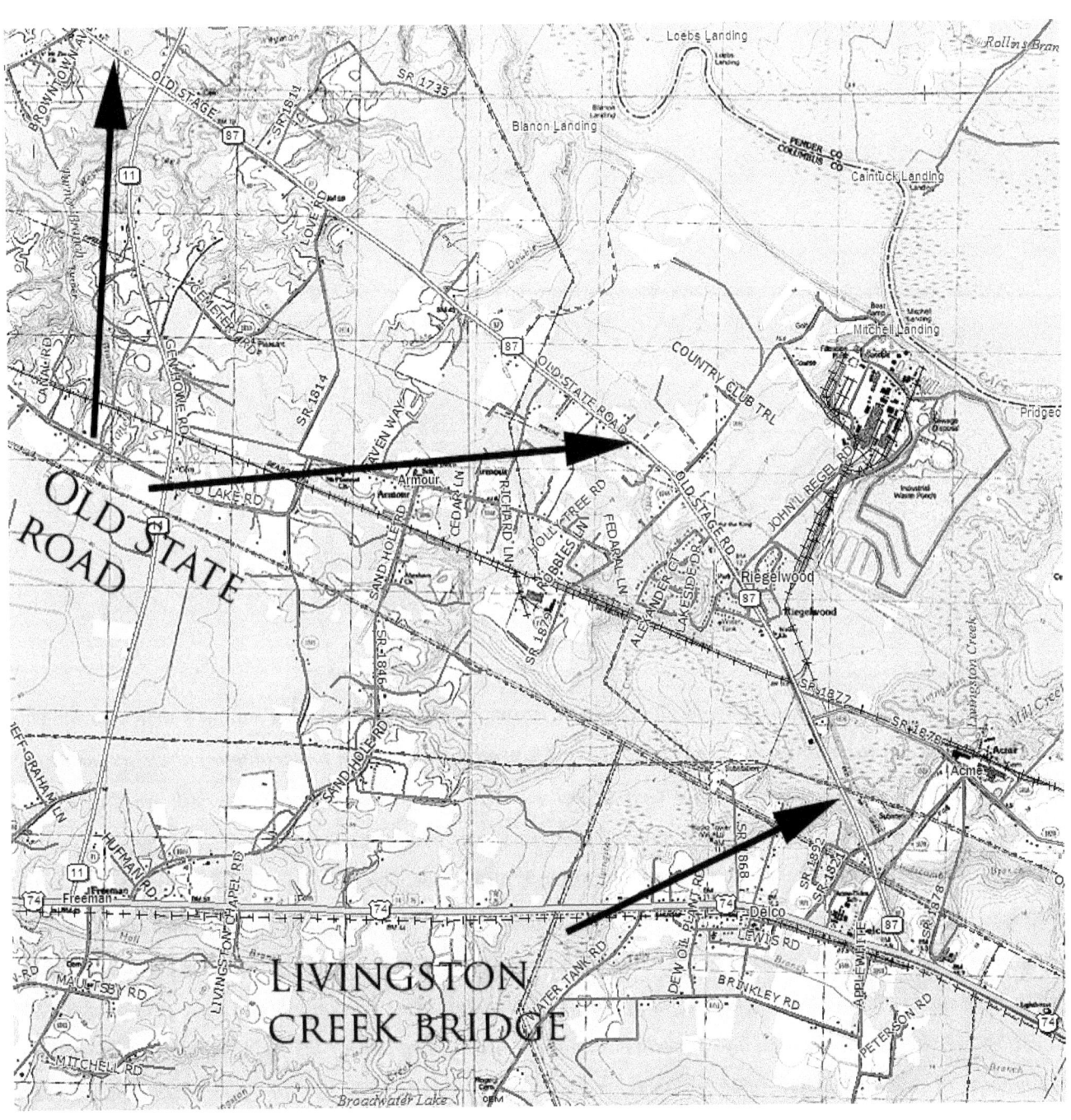

David Williams pension documents that Col Moore brought in reinforcements of 4-500 men. He then details the situation, *"...marched down the Cape Fear to Brown's Ferry...thence they directed their course down the river to Livingston Swamp...had a skirmish with the Tories backed, as was supposed, by about 300 British commanded by Major Craig. A retreat was, on the outset ordered by their commander, which was considered by every brave American as cowardly and shameful. They had their horses about 200 yards in the road of the place where they first formed for battle. When they had retreated to where the horses were tied Colonel Mebane and Brown, with about 150 men, gave the enemy at a sharp returning fire, which threw them into some confusion...The Whigs afterwards rendezvoused at Captain Lucas's, 18 miles from Livingston's Swamp..."* (The map below shows the road crossing Livingston's Creek in 1898)

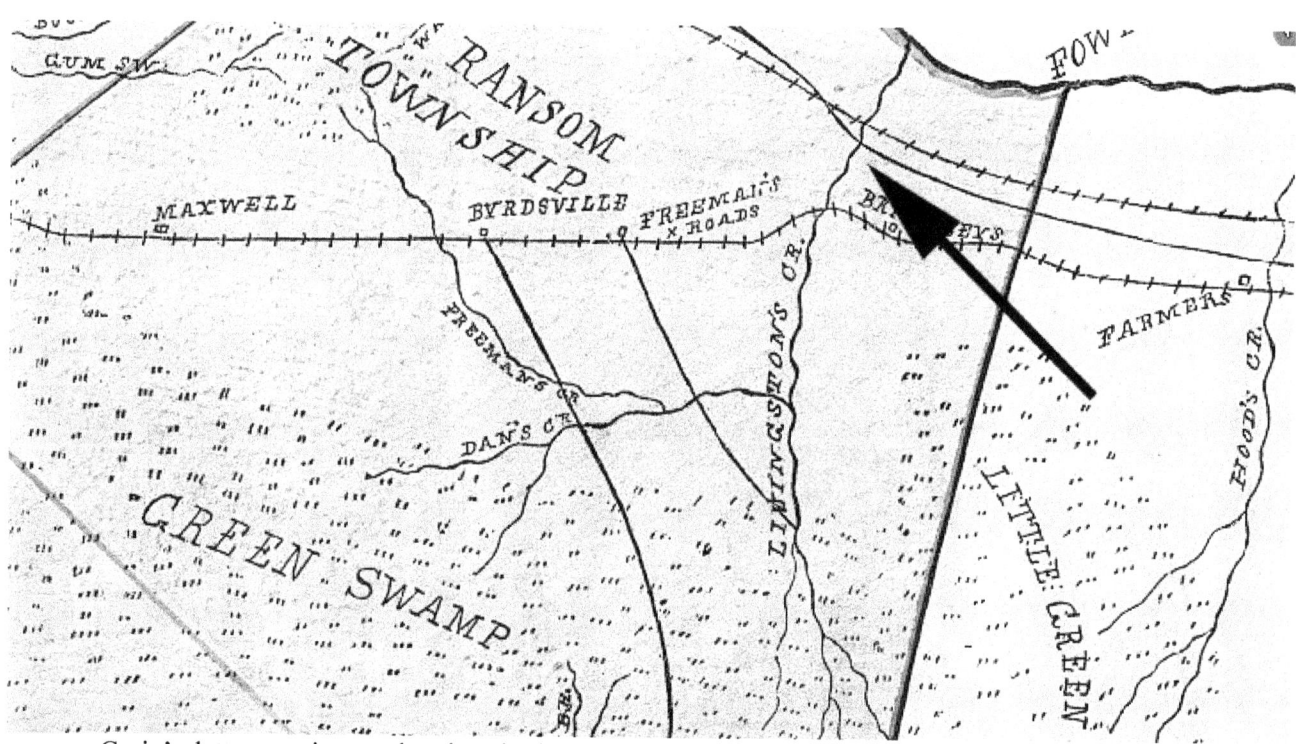

Craig's letter continues, showing the battle at Brown Marsh was to catch Fanning's men returning to their homes, *"When the militia returned I sent Major Manson with 150 men to accompany them as far as the Brown Marsh, we had intelligence that Gen Butler with near six hundred men was still waiting with a determination to intercept them in their return."* Here is a very poignant statement – *"...to intercept them in their return."*, not their entry into Wilmington. That clash already occurred in the prior description. The letter continues, describing the next sequence of events, *"Major Manson getting intelligence of his situation and being apprehensive that if he heard of his being with no time but attack him the moment he could reach him which happened to be at 12 o'clock at night the rebels had accounts of his coming and were prepared for his reception notwithstanding which and notwithstanding the misinformation of his guide which occasioned the whole body of militia that were with him (except about fifty) to be useless, yet the spirit of the officers and men under him overcame every difficulty of numbers and situation, the rebels were completely dispensed leaving twenty dead and five and twenty prisoners, they also a number of wounded who in the darkness of the night got off. We took between 30 and 40 horses but the militia the next day got upwards of a hundred more*

who were running loose in the woods – we had a sergeant and four men wounded one of which is since dead Capt. Holloway of the Orange County militia with one private man killed."

According to other history accounts, the battle happens at Brown Marsh (or swamp) followed by another attempt at Livingston Creek (sometimes called bridge or swamp). But Craig's letter clearly shows the British had escorted the Tories out of Wilmington and had a battle at Brown Marsh around Midnight.

Moab Stevens remembers, *"At the Brown Marsh in September he was in an engagement with the British and Tories combined – that the Army was commanded in that engagement by Gen Butler, Col. Robeson was the commander of his regiment in the three last engagements – and deponent is under the impression the enemy was commanded by Major Craig. In the last mentioned engagement the enemy attacked the Americans in the night time. The American Army was defeated and retreated. The most obstinate part of the fight was sustained by Col Mebane of the Continental Army who was at that time, in the neighborhood and took the command of a detachment..."* Even George Baker said, *"...We joined Gen Butler and pursued the Tories and Scotch and had several skirmishes with them one very warm one at the Brown Marsh..."* Only Walter Brown would recall both battles in his pension, *"...We joined Gen John Butler who commanded as in chief. Gen Butler started with us to Wilmington, and I was engaged in a battle at a place called Livingston's Creek and in another at a place called Brown Marsh, with the British."* This pension corroborates Craig by stating Livingston's occurred first followed by Brown Marsh.

Here are the pensions that document this particular event.

Last Name	First	Location	Who was in command & Misc notes
Barker	George	Brown Marsh	Col. William Moore, Capt John Odham - took place about midnight
Barker	David	Brown Marsh	Caswell Co, under Cap. Oldham and Col Moore, British Troops and Tories Brown Marsh
Bledsoe	Lewis	Brown Marsh	with reinforcements fought at a place called Brown Marsh.
Browning	Robert	Brown Marsh	Butler ordered retreat due to artillary, and there wasn't any
Collins	Eli	Brown Marsh	They had another skirmish near Wimington with the Tories and British
Forrest	James	Brown Marsh	Butler collected with reinforcements not able to overtake due to large British force
Greeen	William	Brown Marsh	Reached Livingstons Bridge about 300 enemy, lasted 15 minutes, retreated
Hargis	Thomas	Brown Marsh	Capt Shadrach Hargis, Gen Butler, somehwere near Wilm. He said Butler fled the battle
Harwell	Andrew	Brown Marsh	Capt White and Gen Butler, mentioned they retreated
Miles (#2)	Thomas	Brown Marsh	Gen Butler, Col Moore, Capt Spillsby Coleman, Lieu James Burton
Mitchell	William	Brown Marsh	crossed river at Browns Ferry, Fanning rec. 300 British under Maj Craig we had 150-200
Pass	Holloway	Brown Marsh	Capt. Adam Sanders, Col William Moore, Col Dudley Reynolds - details
Ray	Francis	Brown Marsh	Under Capt. Adam Sanders, Gov captured, pursued to Brown Marsh, we were defeated
Smith	William	Brown Marsh	Arrived at a swamp, sent 16 spies to find the tories, were captured, but esc during fight
Stevens	Moab	Brown Marsh	Gen Butler and Col Robeson - British and Tories under the command of Major Craig
Thrash	Valentine	Brown Marsh	Col Moore, small engagment with British and Tories at a place called Brown Marsh
Williams	David	Brown Marsh	400 men, Brown's Ferry, Col Moore had 4-500 men, Livingston Swamp, Craig had 300

Off to Wilmington and Prison

Despite all the effort to free the Governor, the remaining band of Tories march their prisoners to Wilmington, N.C. arriving September 24, 1781. This was a very long trip. To march this journey on foot (over 200 miles in the summer) would be a difficult task; one that most people today could not imagine. Governor Burke made this interesting comment about the ordeal, *"I will not trouble you with a relation of the different extremes of hunger, thirst and fatigue, and the frequent dangers our lives were exposed to while we were in the savage hands of those who were our first Captors, who, to avoid the pursuit of our friends, traversed by long and rapid marches, vast pathless tracks of intermingles Sand and Swamp very thinly inhabited and which ought not to be inhabited at all, but will begin with our delivery into the hands of Major Craig on the 23rd of September at Livingston's Creek on the North West of Cape Fear, by which time we were completely pillaged of everything except the few dirty, worthless cloaths [cloths] we had on, which, with regard to myself, were chiefly borrowed."*

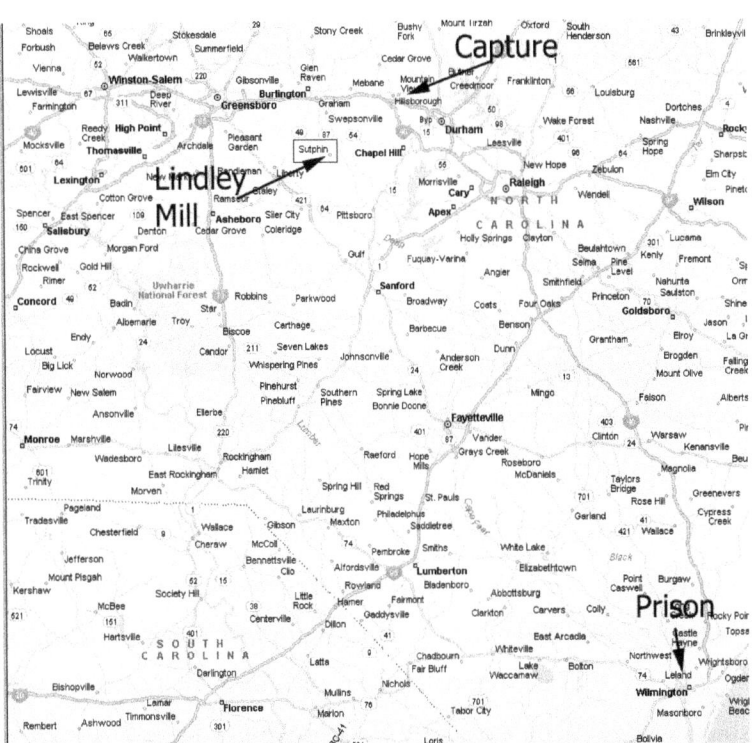

The Tories were clearly treating their prisoners differently than typical British military. This may be attributed to the Tories being a citizen of the area, and taking the war effort to a new level of personal vendetta. Even Gov. Burke recognized this difference and made this statement, *"The British Officers behaved with frank politeness to us and Major Craig treated me with particular respect, in short, we had great reason to rejoice in our exchange of situation, and for the first time after our capture, felt ourselves out of danger of personal violence, with which we had been often threatened, through the savage, ungovernable fury of those people in whose possession we were."* Gov. Burke regarded the Tories ("those people") with disdain.

From this point on, the Patriots were all prisoners of war at a British garrison. Where everyone was placed (housed) is rather difficult to follow, and seemed to vary, depending on rank. Normal military protocol (during the Revolution) utilized a parole process. Typically officers were given a written document which they signed, promising not to escape until they were swapped for like rank (from the opposing side). This version of "house arrest", was for officers only. The common solider would be put in jail, either on land or at sea. There are horrific stories about imprisonment on British prison ships in extremely inhumane conditions. One citizen (on his pension application) stated he was on a British ship for 14 months and was one of the 200 people captured in Hillsborough.

By October 1781, the British surrendered at Yorktown, yet there wasn't any immediate colony-wide surrender or releasing of prisoners. At Yorktown, the commander of the Southern Campaign (Gen Cornwallis) surrendered, and yet the Tory War raged on in the southern states. Even British commander Craig just ignored the surrender and continued to hold prisoners. This was another example of the awful events that continued despite the surrender at Yorktown. Further complicating matters, was the fact that some people captured by Fanning were _not_ in the military, including the Governor. In order to swap prisoners for like prisoners, a problem occurred. The British now held non-military (ranked) personnel. Basically the citizens were arrested like the common criminal yet, (officially) the British Army did not have any authority to arrest a citizen. This caused confusion, and delayed the exchange process for the Governor (and other citizens) - _indefinitely_. The swapping of the military men occurred in a timely manner, yet the "innocent citizens" were left in limbo.

War is hell, and being a prisoners of war, isn't much better. Gov. Burke, in a letter, described the conditions that he witnessed while imprisoned at Wilmington, "*Our prisoner, my dear Sir, by the want of the necessaries of Life in a rigorous confinement call for the assistance and attention of their country at least if I may judge from such as I see daily passing by my window to the spring for water, which well be taken for skeletons, did they not retain life enough to make them appear to ghastly and some languid unanimated motion that show they have some small remains of strength.*"

In a letter written to Gen Greene by Col Lytle on December 27, 1781 he states, (the following quote includes notes from the authors of Nathanael Greene Papers, Vol 10) "*Despite his [Col Lytle] status as a paroled prisoner, he was confined, very much wounded by Fanning and taken to Wilmington where he was turned over to Major Craig. Lytle informed Craig of his situation and identified the people who had his horses, but to none effect. He has explained his situation to every officer, into whose charge he has come since leaving North Carolina, but nothing has been done. Because he refuses to sign another parole unless a satisfactory cause is given for his second capture, confinement and inhuman treatment, he expects this day to be ordered into close confinement. The officers have not been allowed servants since our departure from Cape Fear; since their arrival in town [Charleston S.C.] neither servants quarters nor rations have been assigned to them.*" Here is more proof (from another person's view) of how the British were ignoring the requests of certain (key or influential) men, not just Gov. Burke.

A long and complicated story shortened, Governor Burke (now separated from his fellow prisoners) was moved from Wilmington, N.C., to Charleston, S.C. then on to Sullivan's Island. Burke complained that he did not belong at a military fort (Arbuthnot was located on Sullivan Island), and that it was not conducive for his parole. The British moved him to James Island. It was on James Island that he was paroled to a home. This island had some interesting people residing on it. Descriptions by those who visited included; "filthy", and "cut throats". One officer stated, "[he]...*would sooner go into a dungeon than take a parole on that Island in its present situation..*". Once the word was out, that a rebel governor was in a particular home, these barbarous people started to shoot randomly through the windows at whoever was inside. Burke stated that British officers (patrolling the area) had a difficult time controlling those with firearms. Burke wrote the British commander asking for a safer location, and they ignored his request. He determined to make his escape, thus breaking parole (breaking a man's promise in the 18th century, was not well accepted or respected). After he escapes, these scrupulous people shot at the house again, supposing to be shooting at the Governor, instead, injuring those inside.

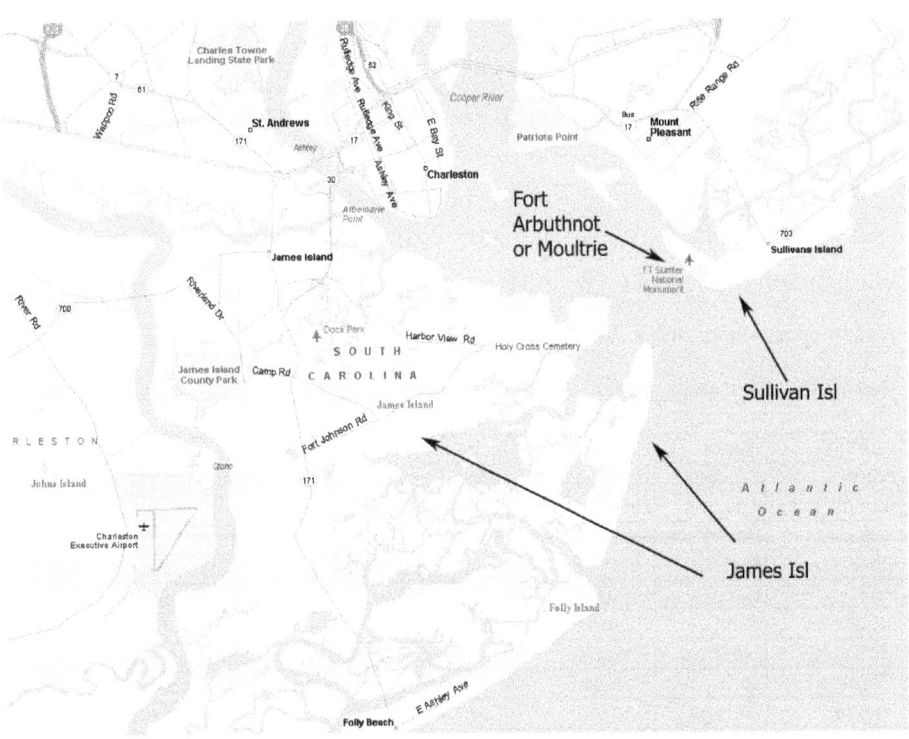

One of the reasons the British did not want to release Governor Burke, was that (British) Gen. Leslie swore that Burke would retaliate and have Fanning and his fellow loyalist arrested, and killed. Another interesting letter was from Major Craig writing his superiors about Gov Burke, N.C. Archives, British Records, 1781 – X/L05252), *"…Mr. Burke and all the Continentals officers with regard to the former I must beg to make a remark, that he is by far the man of the greatest abilities and one of the most violent in the Province – a man whose principles will I believe never interfere with his projects and who if exchanged is capable of doing infinite mischief in these parts where I assure you the turn for toryism or rebellion partly near on a pair [on par] or in point of numbers certainly in favor of the former in this situation his being exchanged is a matter of infinite consequence to the kind of war carrying on here & I must most strenuously request to put an absolute negative if possible but at all wants to delay it as long as possible."* Here is proof that Burke's delay in being paroled or released was well planned by the British. Why? – *"…capable of doing infinite mischief…"*, leading the rebellion against the British was certainly mischief making, in their view. Burke never knew the British were the reason for his delayed release. He thought his fellow officers and statesmen had ignored his situation, while in prison. This would eventually cause him to be soured, and vows never to hold any *public office* again. In addition, breaking "his oath" in the 18th century would become a political nightmare, as it was used against him. Others criticized his lack of honor. Yet, the day after he escapes, he goes back to work as Governor, and continues to work against the British stranglehold on the State.

You can be sure that every effort was made to capture Fanning. In a letter from Capt. William O'Neal to Gov. Burke, March 19, 1782 stating that, *"On the 16th day of Sept. last, General Butler dismissed me from under his immediate command with orders to return to Orange County and to endeavor, by every possible means, to apprehend Fanning, who was wounded at the battle of Lindley's Mill and left behind."* They never did capture him, and Fanning continued his attacks, more brutal than ever; shooting individual men (in the head) that were Patriots; burning their homes to the ground; almost a get-even campaign, while he waited for an official surrender (Treaty of Paris in 1783). He eventually leaves the state, unharmed.

And the other prisoners?

As mentioned earlier, it is very difficult to track all the prisoners captured by David Fanning. Gov Burke wrote a letter November 26, 1781 to the "acting Governor" Martin from James Island *"I am informed that my fellow prisoners who had been paroled to Beaufort are arrived in Charlestown…"*. This letter clearly documents that some of the prisoners were paroled.

Albright	Henry	Prisoner	Capt James Trousdale, Lieu John Campbell - prison ship abt 11mnths - July 1782
Allen	William	Prisoner	Archibald Lytle, exchanged 8/11/1782 - on a ship
Allman	Edward	Prisoner	Gave no information
Austin	Benjamin	Prisoner	Capt. Abraham Allen, Col Hugh Teenan, escaped during transfer of prisons Apr 9, 1782
Christmas	Richard	Prisoner	Prison ship Eske, exch for Capt. Osbourn July 1, 1782
Fox	Gatus	Prisoner	Lytle, prisoner for 3 mths, sent to prison - "Provo"
Matthews	John	Prisoner	He said that he was captured "on their way" and McKay parolled him before Wilmington
McCauley	Matthew	Prisoner	Lieu Archibald Lytle - 6 months on Eske
Mebane	John	Prisoner	Prison Ship for several weeks exch for Lieu McClain
Neese	George	Prisoner	Capt John Clendenin, Wilmington to Eske to Charleston - July 1782 release
Turner	James	Prisoner	Taken across Woody's Ferry, then to Stallworth, then Lindley's, then on Eske

A pension record of William Allen stated that he was a prisoner (he was a soldier in prior years serving under Col. Lytle in Hillsborough) and was put on board a British ship which ultimately was anchored in Charleston, and was released August 11, 1782. Also John Mebane, brother of Col Robert Mebane, was a prisoner along with his neighbor, and close friend, William Kinchen. John stated, they too, were put on a prison ship at Wilmington and from there sailed to Charleston, S.C., where *"they were still confined on board the ship for a long time, suffering from extremely by the privations, heat, filth and vermin and the diseases common on board prison-ships."* The story continued that when released, William Kinchen dies on the way home. John Mebane marries William Kinchen's widow. Several pension records clearly document the ship's name was – Eske. Researching this ship via the internet has uncovered nothing. In fact, another researcher stated he too could not find any information about this ship. Searching the PRO records in the State Archives (Raleigh) cataloging all HMS (His Majesty's Ships) vessels, did not document the Eske. All that was discovered was that Eske is a village-name in England. One pension record, written by a widow (Matthew McCauley #W17121) stated – *"She remembers the name of the vessel very well, as she has frequently heard her husband speak of the hardships he suffered on board of said prison ship. She said he was release either the first day of March or April of 1782."* Pension of James Turner document the route the prisons took, *"…this applicant, his captain and most of his company [John Clendennin] with many of were made prisoners and carried to the south, crossing Haw River, at Woody's Ferry – the first nigh we were taken to Stallworth's a little this side of Lindley's Mill on Cain Creek. The next morning the Tories holding us prisoners were attacked at said mills by some of our forces under Gen Butler and Col Mebane and others – we were hurried on to Wilmington in this State where we were put on board a British brig and were confined some weeks, when we were conveyed by said to Charleston South Carolina and put on board as prisoners of war, a British vessel called the 'Eske' where this applicant remained in close confinement till sometime in the month of April following, when through the friendly interference of his Captain john Clendenin he was released from his imprisonment and returned home about the first of May 1782."*

Postlude

Liberate Wilmington?

Nothing has been written about an effort to free Burke, another missed piece of history (pertaining to Burke). In the Green Papers, are a series of letters documenting Gen Nathanael Greene's attempt to attack the British at Wilmington. The first letter was addressed to Gen George Washington (October 7, 1781 – Greene was in Charlotte) *"…I had it in contemplation to lay siege to Wilmington and was taking measures with Governor Burke for the purpose when unfortunately he was very unexpectedly made a prisoner by a party of Tories. Our force is much too small to attempt what seems absolutely necessary to be done, but if your Army comes southerly the work will soon be accomplished…"* James Iredell, when writing his wife (Hannah), he stated that Burke was planning something big, but did not know what it entailed. This letter clearly documents that it was a planned attack to rout the British from Wilmington. Maj Craig's free reign in N.C. (supporting and supplying all the Tory forces) was nothing but detrimental to the war effort. Greene writes Gen Washington again, (October 25, 1781), *"…concerting with Governor Burke a plan for the reduction of Wilmington, Gen Rutherford is moving down towards that place with a considerable body of Militia and I hear the enemy have left the place and now occupy Brunswick 30 miles below…preparations making in Charles Town of small transports…"* Washington replies, (October 31, 1781) *"…French fleet should be sent to liberate Wilmington or Charles Town…"*. History documents the French (Comte de Grasse) disagreed to execute any military campaign on either town. Neither did Gen Washington send any of his troops south to liberate either city.

Despite this, Gen Greene continues to discuss the effort. He writes (acting) Gov Martin (November 14, 1781) *"…The expulsion of the enemy from Wilmington is an object for may reasons much to be wished; and is what I have long in contemplation and more than once held detachments in readiness for the purpose. But the smallness of my force together with Gov. Burkes unexpected misfortune has obliged me to lay to aside…"* Was Greene concerned the British would kill Burke if he attacked?

Never the less, by November (Nov. 25), the British leave Wilmington and move towards Charles Town.

Governor Burke – return to office

After his escape from James Island, he returns home and his letters start back up, as well as letters written to him, welcoming him back. In the brief historical accounts of his life, most state that upon arrival back home everyone was so upset with him over breaking parole. Here are the letters that took an opposite view;

- R. Bignall – Tarborough, February 13, 1782 – *"I have just heard of your being in Halifax. Be assured I do sincerely congratulate you on your safe arrival to your family and Government."*
- P.Mallett – Wilmington, February 1782 – *"I never could hear of your arrival in the State until yesterday. I cannot well express my feelings on the news."*
- Wm McCauley – New Hope, February 10, 1782 – *"I take the pleasure in writing you, in the first place giving you joy for your deliverance out of the hands of the enemy and also taking the reins of government that through you peace may be handed down to us and our children after us upon honorable terms."*

Upon his return to office, Gov. Burke wrote Gen Leslie on January 8, 1782, which was the British commander who he wrote earlier (while a prisoner) to tell about his danger, and was ignored. He wrote him again re-reminding him of the events that led up to his escape, and then ends with this, *"I will endeavor to procure for you a just and reasonable equivalent in exchange for me, or if that cannot be effected, I will return within your lines on parole, provided, you will pledge your honor that I shall not be treated in any manner different from the officers of the Continental Army when prisoners of War."* (Again, remember that Cornwallis has surrendered, the British were defeated!)

Gen. Leslie writes Gen. Greene on January 27, 1782 asking for Gov. Burkes return, *"I am convinced you would never intentionally give any encouragement or countenance to the violation of a parole, tho' the person acting so contrary to character of a gentleman had some excuse to palliate his conduct. I flatter myself, Sir, you are so sensible of the great impropriety, not to give it a harsher appellation of Governor Burke's conduct, that you will immediately order him to return and deliver himself up to the Commissary in Charlestown, where he will be assured of every protection. The reason for Mr. Burke has attempted to advance his vindication being so totally chimerical, that I cannot give the smallest credit to them, nor consider them as motives for his conduct."* Then Gen. Greene responds February 1, 1782, *"I have received your letter concerning Governor Burke, and although I cannot justify the violation of parole, yet I am not agreed with you in opinion that his apprehensions where chimerical, for Col. Washington says he would sooner go into a dungeon than take a parole on that Island in its present situation; and what serves to confirm me in opinion, that the danger was far greater than you apprehended, is some violence's latterly committed upon your officers at the Waxhaws the authors of which, can they be discovered, shall be punished with the utmost severity, and was it not a matter of civil resort, could be detected, should suffer immediate death. Gov. Burke is gone to North Carolina, and before I can write him fully on this subject I wish to know in what light you consider him, whether a prisoner of War, or as Major Craig affects to hold him a State Prisoner."* Then he writes Gov. Burke on February 5 and states, *"Since you left this place, Gen'l Leslie has demanded your immediate return. Enclosed is a copy of his letter and my answer by which you will see upon* what footing the business rests. I expect to hear from him again in a day or two. Should he agree to the proposition that I have made, and exchanges go on again, I shall propose yours. But whatever may be the issue I will inform you freely."

After this letter from Gen. Greene, nothing was found that documented what Gen. Leslie's reply was (to Gen. Greene). It was a letter dated March 18, 1782 from Gen. Greene to Gov. Burke that stated he never heard from Gov. Burke on Gen Leslie's reply, "*I have received your letters of the 31st of January and of the 15th and 22nd of February and as you mentioned nothing of the receipt of my letter inclosing General Leslie's answer, I herewith inclose [enclosed] you copies.*" In this letter we get more of Gen. Greene's view of what needs to be done, " *I advised you to return to your Government and wait General Leslie's answer. My advice was intended to place your conduct in as favorable a point of light as possible. I wish your engaging in business may not give your enemies both at home and abroad some occasion to sport with your feeling. I am sensible how necessary your serves are both for the interests of your State and this Army, but whatever inconveniences I might have felt from <u>your remaining out of office</u>, I should rather have undergone them than demand your aid on terms not perfectly honorable to yourself. Your zeal to serve me and the Army under my command claims my warmest acknowledgements nor shall any thing on my part be wanting to effect your exchange. I have made two essays since you left me, but neither succeeded, and at both of which they peremptorily demanded your return to captivity. Captain Shubrick, who made the last, was instructed to demand Governor Wright if they demanded you and to offer him in exchange, but not to rest it on that footing, if he could effect it by any other composition. However nothing was done, and another meeting is to take place in five or six days. Thus you see how the business has circumstanced, and your own feelings must govern your conduct, in matters so truly delicate and interesting to yourself. The enemy seems to know your importance and I fear will embarrass your exchange on that account. Many people in Charles Town justify your first escape from the dangerous situation you was placed in ; and I have heard that the morning after you left James Island a man was shot at the door of your quarters on the presumption of it being you.*" This letter is very clear about Gen. Greene's views, as some historian poignantly state Greene disliked Burke, and wanted him to go back to prison. <u>This is not true.</u>

General Greene writes to Gov. Burke on April 8, 1782 "*Your letter of the 5th of March came to hand a few days since. I am very sorry if anything has been said by Colonel Williams or by anybody else that has made your situation painful. The Col, had no authority from me to say anything on the subject. My advice to you was dictated by the purest motives of private friendship and public good. It was my wish that you should do nothing that should give an opening to reflect on you, either in your private or public capacity. The measure I advised you to, I though, was founded on justice, and perfectly consistent with the dignity of your public character. That your life was in danger seems to be generally agreed to and that after you took measures for its security your proposition carried the strongest evidence that it was an act of necessity and not of choice, and that you was willing to do justice to the Enemy's claims upon you if their operation could be limited to Military propriety. If any censure can happen to you it is from engaging in business before the* *matter was fully settled between you and General Leslie. It is very difficult to make people think liberally which renders more delicacy and circumspection necessary. Good intentions are not always, a full security against censure because they are not always sufficiently known."*

Finally on April 12, 1782 Gov. Burke writes Gen Greene, *"I am exceedingly obliged to you for the interest you take in my affair which has given me more uneasiness than any other incident in my life because of my apprehensions lest I should not find it practicable to convey just ideas of the circumstances, and consequently the malicious may find room to attribute my conduct to improper motives, a fate I fear, It will no possible be for me to avoid. As to what may follow should the enemy inflexibly insist on my return, they will probably lose thereby every advantage from my capture."* This portion of the letter is important, in order to understand his feelings about the situation. The letter continues with another regurgitation over the events that occurred. Then he makes this amazing comment, *"They unfortunately place a higher value on me than my own country did, but a little more time will make me of no value of either, except as a mere obscure individual, for I am preparing as fast as possible to take a final leave of all public business, happy that our affairs are in so promising a situation that I can indulge my inclination for retirement without giving room to suppose that I am moved by apprehensions for our success."* It seems that he has had enough, and his comments allude that even at home there is a negative view about his conduct. How quickly they forgot his prior efforts! As near as can be determined (from all these letters), the British must have given up on their request or his loss of reelection was sufficient for them to drop the issue.

How did Governor Burke feel about all these issues? Supposedly with all the public comments (although none found in any paper) about breaking parole coupled with the issues he personally faced, it seemed that he was really disheartened by it all. In a talk he gave to General Assembly on April 16, 1782, he gave them his recount of what he went through and then annunciated his feelings, *"Tho' I was confined as a prisoner of State, and that particularly avowed, and published, and though our Arms were triumphant and our power unquestioned, not the least regard was paid to my situation, no effort was made even to procure me the treatment of a prisoner of war and I was left to subsist as I could though plundered of everything. Congress has also refused to give in exchange for me any but the citizens taken at York a people who the enemy are so far from wishing to regain that they are already burthened [burdened] with a useless train of them, This was certainly equivalent to a negative and if founded either in justice or utility is incomprehensible to me."* A little further he stated *"I am happy that this conduct has no such excuse, and I take the liberty of a freeman to say that it was both unwise and unworthy and far from that degree of respect to which the State whose Magistrate I had the honor to be is entitled."* Finally he closed with this last jab, *"I do not expect to be so fortunate as that every one will judge candidly of an affair so circumstanced as this I have related and I am aware that some men felt no concern for me while in captivity and who would have been very easy had I been murdered have taken some malicious liberties on the subject of my escape, but I hope for the fair and candid decision of the General Assembly to whom only I deem myself accountable and I forbear to lay before you any correspondence on the subject in the order that the opinions you give may be unquestionably your own on a plain statement of circumstances.*" Even at this time it was clear what he wanted to do "*...I hope I shall be permitted to return to a more private life which is so necessary to my affairs. Thomas Burke.*"

Tuesday, April 12, 1782 the General Assembly met, and the following message was read, which is Gov. Burke's, letter to remove his name from the balloting for Governor, "*This afternoon is appointed for the election of Governor, and I am in nomination. Permit me to say it was my wish that the several Intimations I have given the General Assembly might have prevented any gentleman from naming me as a candidate for an office which I sincerely wish to be filled by a much abler man, or be any man rather than myself. When the General Assembly did me then honor to make choice of me for their Chief Magistrate, tho' nothing could be more injurious to me or more repugnant to my inclinations, I accepted the trust because I was apprehensive that declining it would be construed into a doubt of our success, which at a time when our prospects were overcast, might have had bad consequences. Happily, that reason no longer exists, and I do not now feel the necessity of sacrificing my time and industry, which are absolutely necessary to retrieve my private affairs from the ruin in which my being constantly employed in public several years has very nearly involved them. My misfortunes during this year have been heavy and complicated and have involved me in debts and in private distresses which it would be painful to particularize. I hope it may be sufficient to say that it will require the best exertions of my industry to extricate me from them. Tho' I could offer many other reasons, I hope they are unnecessary and that what I have said will sufficiently justify my request that my name be struck out of the nomination. As this will, I presume, be the last message I shall have the honor to send the General Assembly I hope I shall be indulged in requesting that they may point out some mode whereby I am to settle my accounts, for such applications as I have made of the monies voted for the Contingencies of Government during my Administration, and of such other supplies have fallen under my direction ; Also to inform me whether I am to consider the advances made on my credit to the citizens of this State when prisoners with the Enemy, are to be ultimately borne by the public or myself. Through several of my vouchers I fear are lost through the destruction of my papers by the enemy, yet I had rather suffer the loss of Sums they may be for than leave unsettled accounts and give the least color for ranking me in the number of public defaulters.*"

Thomas Burke never had a complete term in office, he spent about as much time in office as he did as a prisoner, and it is a shame we never got to see how well he would have performed his duty without this unfortunate event.

November 1782 the British agreed to American Independence and made a <u>preliminary accord</u> with America. In January of 1783 they signed the <u>preliminary</u> peace treaty, with France and Spain, On April 14th, the Governor of New Jersey issued a Proclamation that ended formal hostilities. It was the **Treaty of Paris** that was signed September 3, 1783 that <u>officially ended the war</u>. The British were still in New York City. Not until November 23, 1783 were the British to leave the City. To most historians, Washington riding into New York City with the remainder of the army (most had been furloughed) is the end of the war. At Fraunces Tavern,

Washington took leave of his officers, asking each to come and take his hand. It was an emotional moment for them all a bittersweet parting, the breaking of a fellowship.

Thomas left public office on April 1782 and remained at home, and according to his resignation letter, to put his private life back in order. There were some letters that referenced Thomas Burke, dealing with law, so it is assumed, he went back to his law career. The first letter written was April 1, 1783, from the Hon. Samuel Johnston from Hayes, N.C. discussing legal issues and at the bottom under a P.S. he stated that Mr. Culun Edwards had requested Thomas to be retained for a law suit in Halifax.

In another letter written to Thomas Burke illustrating how Gen. Nathanael Greene really thought about Thomas, written October 29, 1782, *"That you can retire from humble life with honor I never had a doubt; but I can by no means be satisfied that you should. Your State and indeed all the Southern States require many singularities and improvements to render Civil government perfect. Few men have the necessary abilities and still fewer a proper degree of industry to effect it."* Then he continues with his views about the nation, *"Unless our government are rendered more perfect and our union more complete, I fear we shall not feel but in a negative way the blessings we expect from independence. Think not, therefore, of retiring soon."* This letter was both insightful to Gen. Greene's view of issues still facing America, as well as his complete confidence in Thomas Burke, and his abilities!

Officially he receives notice that he has been "exchanged" and it first came from his friend and fellow prisoner Col. Arch. Lytle on October 25, 1782, *"I have not the time or paper to be as full and explicit in my intelligence to you as I could wish. You are exchanged with all those captured on this side the Delaware in a Civil or Militia character prior to the 24th of October 1782."* Also Gen Greene states on the 29th of October, *"I have the pleasure to inform you of your exchange. The mode will be published in the papers. It was with difficulty we got you included, but as the Enemy could not get the other advantages which I held up to them, without consenting to that, they at last agreed, after many shifts and evasions."* Then he continues, *"If in effecting your exchange I have done you a service, I am happy and have only to wish you may find it more consistent with your feeling, though not with your interest, still to lend you aid to accomplish the freedom and Independence of the United States rather than to retire into private life."*

The very last letter, on record, being written by Thomas was dated November 9, 1783 from Edenton. It is a lengthy letter and his handwriting is very difficult to read, and begins, *"Your letter of June 30th I should have acknowledge earlier, had not a fierce illness which had nearly proved fatal, prevented me."* Here we have some insight as to the beginning of the illness in the summer, and he is now getting around to responding, but at the very end of the letter we learn more, *"I must beg of you to excuse me for the presence of my health is still very infirm and writing is very painful to me."* (This letter is on microfilm, roll #2 of the UNC Southern Collection.)

Thomas Burke passed away at his home December 3, 1783 at age 36. What a tragic end, and a waste of talent. Thomas Burke would have been even more famous, had he survived. Was he missed? Here are some comments from the infamous two men, with a lot of letters between them, Hon. A. Maclaine to George Hooper dated March 25, 1783, now three months after Thomas died, and he states; *"Caswell, as I expected is a candidate for the Government. He does not deserve it. I also suspect Nash, who is returned from Congress. But I think he has no chance of succeeding. The present Governor has, I am persuaded, expectations. I wish we could have better than any of them. But I do not know whether Mr. Johnson is in the Assembly. <u>O! how I wish for Burke with all his foibles. He would keep villains within proper bounds, and call scoundrels to a strict account; but probably these are the very reasons they make against his election.</u>"* Most historians state, it was over breaking parole!

Another letter, written by William Hooper to James Iredell (Hillsborough, Jan 4, 1784) *"…Dr. Burke died about a fortnight since, and fell, in some measure, a sacrifice to the obstinacy which marked his character through life. Had he declined his journey to Edenton, he might have been alive. It would, however, be a question with his friends whether life upon the terms he had it would not have been a curse in the extreme. Laboring under a complication of disordered oppressed with the most agonizing pains, which for months had deprived him of his natural rest; his whole mass of blood dissolved; his temper soured with disappointment; and, to sum up his misery, no domestic prop to lean upon – no friend or companion, as his own home, to soothe the anguish of his mind, or mitigate his paid of body – was not death to him "a comforter, friend, and physician? He carried his indifference to his wife to the grave with him. By his will he has left nothing absolutely at her disposal. He has devised to her an estate for life – not half of his estate; and, upon her marriage, has restrained, and curtailed that in some degree."* Then he mentions about the debt, *"…Burke's debt, I fear, will swallow up the whole."* Hooper ends with this comment about Burke's slaves, *"…Burke has denied all the Negroes but one as his own property*." (See Life and Correspondence of James Iredell, Vol 2 page 83-84 for the complete letter)

(Gov. Burke's grave site, September 2006)

Col Robert Mebane

Family tradition states that on his way back from Brown Marsh that Col Mebane was killed. In fact the story states *"On the way, he came upon a noted Tory and horse thief by the name of Henry Hightower, who was armed with a British musket. Knowing him, and perhaps too fearless and regardless of consequences, he pursued him and when within striking distance with his arm uplifted, Hightower wheeled and shot him."* Caruthers states that – *"It was on his return from this expedition that he was killed..."* The "return" was returning from the final engagement at Brown Marsh. In a pension record of William C. Smith (S3924) he states, *"...Your applicant was discharged by his Captain Lewis Bledsoe....and on their way home Col Mabane his Captain and several others was going on to Wake County where they all lived they came across a Tory in an old field who Col Mabane knew and the Col swore he would take him or his life. He charged upon him and the Tory broke and run and Col Mabane after him on horse through the old field in the field there was a gully and some grape vines had grown over it Colonel Mabane went to charge the gully and his horse got entangled in it and fell and threw him. The Tory turned and shot Col Mabane as he was getting up and killed him. We buried Col Mabane and this applicant returned home to Wake County North Carolina..."*

Researching Henry Hightower, County records document that he was tried (in court) as a horse thief, and found guilty, *"April 8, 1783 in Hillsborough District Court – State vs. Henry Hightower, horse thief, he pleaded not guilty. He was found guilty and sentenced to be hanged by the Sheriff of Orange County between 10 A.M. and 4 P.M. on April 18, 1783."* Note the trial date (1783), although Mebane was killed in 1781. Was Hightower's actions considered a military engagement, so that Mebane was a war victim therefore not a "murder"? Never the less, this was the end of Hightower, and this court case doesn't document that he was to be hanged for murder. Henry Hightower was born in Orange County (1763) and lived in Chatham County. He was mentioned in his dad's will written in 1782, and probated in 1784 (Chatham County). To take this further, I found in a letter from British Maj. Craig (N.C. Archives, British Records, 1781 – X/L05252 – 79.1890.1) dated November 6, 1781, *"...Fanning who is just recovering from his wound is again the terror of the Country seven of his men lately killed a Colonel Mebane (a Continental Colonel much esteemed) & six others; many of the Militia of the lower part have from terror joined Rutherford at which I am very glad, as they will never do him any good..."* Here is a documented report from the British, stating a different situation, in that it was more like a skirmish or even a trap, but was *not* a one-on-one fight. Would Craig be making up a story? Was Fanning reporting a lie? Finally, there are a number of internet postings that state Col Robert Mebane died at Yorktown – not hardly.

David Fanning

Governor Burke established an effort to round up the Tories in the local area, and try to get someone to capture Fanning. Ultimately the war ends, due to the Treaty of Paris (October 1783), much later than the surrender of Cornwallis to Washington (October 1781). Governor Burke receives a letter from William

McCauley and Abraham Allen, New Hope, February 10, 1782 asking for two prisoners (Tories) to be forgiven. *"I shall further take the liberty of petitioning your Excellency concerning four unhappy persons now in Hillsborough jail under condemnation, who are to be executed the first day of next month unless your Excellency should interfere."* He was asking for two of the four (unhappy) to be forgiven, Thomas Estridge and Merdeth Edwards. The four to be hanged included (beside the prior two names), Thomas Dark, Thomas Ricketts. Abraham states *"Capt. Allen begs to be remembered to your Excellency and also his wound has got well, and would further say that if it had not been for Estridge, Horn, others would have killed him that day your Excellency was taken."* As near as can be determined (based on the next letter), only three of the four were hanged.

Fanning was upset by this situation, and on February 29, 1782, he writes Governor Burke. (Imagine writing a former captor, and now back in power as Governor – demanding and threatening!) Fanning writes, *"I understand that you have hung three of my men, one Captain and two privates and likewise have a Captain and six men under the death sentence. Sir, if the requisition of my articles do not arrive to satisfaction and the effusion of blood stopped and the lives of those men save, that I will retaliated blood for blood and tenfold for one and there shall never and officer or private of the rebel party escape that falls into my hand hereafter but what shall suffer the pain and punishment of instant death."* This letter was very lengthy, as David continued his rant to the Governor (State Records Vol 16 page 205-207). Nothing has been found that documented the disposition of this "stand off". The war was nearing its end, and David Fanning would – walk away! Fanning documents in his memoirs, that he was involved in 36 skirmishes in the state of N.C., and many of his men survived the ordeal without punishment for their vigilante work, burning homes, and murdering men – despite Cornwallis' surrender to Gen Washington, thus ending the British Southern Campaign. Fanning continued to kill and burn, many months later.

David Fanning (admitted in his book) sought out revenge in one particular situation. Another example of the tenacity (and bitterness) between those impelled to fight based on personal feelings, than purely a military action (such as attempting to get a surrender), which is somewhat less personal. David wrote, *"In the course of this correspondence, endeavoring to make peace, I had reason to believe they did not intend to be as good as their words; as three of their people followed Capt. Linley [Lindley]; and cut him to pieces with their swords. I was immediately informed of it, and kept a look out for them. Five days after their return, I took two [of] them and hung them, <u>by way of retaliation</u>, both on the same limb of the same tree ; the third made his escape."* It is true the men who killed Lindley were not following procedures either, and proves the "war" was much more than a military engagement, it was a *civil war*. If both sides focused on capture and imprisonment, it would be more military-like. But towards the end, Fanning was specifically targeting key people, all the while knowing that his days were numbered, since Cornwallis' surrender.

When Fanning learned that British General Leslie, was soon to evacuate Charlestown (a sign the British were really going to surrender), Fanning lashed out a few more times before making his way to Charlestown arriving September 28, *"..where the shipping was ready for me to embark for St. Augustine."* North Carolina was finally rid of Tory Fanning and he was off to Spanish territory - Florida!

The Loyalist

- Col. Edmund Fanning – Moved to Prince Edward Island, Canada and was made lieutenant governor for his services in the Revolutionary War. (not related to David below)

- Col. David Fanning – Initially he moved (PRO – AO 13, ERD/7674) to St. Augustine Florida (July 15, 1783 to March 25, 1784) From there he moved to New Brunswick, Canada. He was elected three times to the provincial assembly of New Brunswick from 1791 to 1801. Then they moved to Digby, Nova Scotia, where he died March 14, 1835.

- Col. Banastre Tarelton – Remained in the Army and eventually made the rank of General. However, after leaving America, he never led his men into combat. Later in life he served in Parliament.

- Major John Raines – moved to Tennessee and was a poor miller, and still alive in 1819. His dad, John Rains Sr. was killed at Lindley's Mill during the battle.

- Capt. Daniel McNeil – moved to Nova Scotia

- Col Arch. McDugald – He moved to Nova Scotia, then to England and obtained a pension and ultimately returns to N.C. and raised a respectable family.

- John McLean – He was in charge of Gov Burke during his capture and settled on the lower Cape Fear, near the Bluff Church, under the protection of a Whig friend.

- Alexander McKay – died a wealthy man in the West Indies.

- Col Duncan Ray – moved to Nova Scotia

- Gen Lord Cornwallis – Governor of East Indies in 1786, Lord Lieutenant of Ireland in 1798, Gov General of India in 1804 and died at Ghazepoore 1805.

- Edward Family – Richard Edwards was killed at Kirk's Farm a week before Lindleys Mill, Edward Edwards dies in the battle, and Merdeth Edwards was hung in Hillsborough in 1782.

- Maj. James Craig - became Governor General of Upper Canada after more war efforts in South Africa etc. He too, dies in Canada.

Here is another important North Carolina battle (during the American Revolution) emphasizing the struggle for independence costing many lives. It also serves to illustrate the amazing stamina our early forefathers embodied, including a clear sense of duty to their Country. Let us never forget, as we pledge our allegiance to the flag of the United States of America, what sacrifices were made for our freedom.

Further Reading

The Battle of Lindley's Mill – Algie I. Newlin.

Pyle's Defeat: Deception at the Racepath – Carole Watterson Troxler

The Battle of Guilford Courthouse – Berthold Koch

North Carolina in the American Revolution – Hugh F. Rankin

Breaking Loose Together, The Regulator Rebellion – Marjoleine Kars

The North Carolina Continentals – Hugh F. Rankin

Prelude to Yorktown – M.F. Treacy

The Complete History of Thomas Burke – Stewart Dunaway

Civil War in the American Revolution – Stewart Dunaway

The Battle at Clapp's Mill – Stewart Dunaway and Jeffery Bright

Pyle's Defeat – Stewart Dunaway and Jeffery Bright

The Battle at Weitzel's Mill – Stewart Dunaway

The Battle at Hart's Mill – Stewart Dunaway

Like a Bear with his Stern in a Corner – Bright/Dunaway

Life and Correspondence of James Iredell Vol 1 and Vol 2 – McRee (1858)

Appendix A – Pension notes

1. James Clark #?????? – Butler and Mebane- engaged at Lindley's Mill - Whereupon the army recrossed the river and marched up the same to Cane Break where we met the Tories under the command of Colonels Fanning and McNeill and engaged them near Lindley's Mills. The action commenced about breakfast time in thick woods. The American foot retreated in disorder early in the engagement, but the horse, 77 strong under the command of Colonel Mebane, maintained their ground until they had given them eleven fires when their ammunition failed and they were forced to retreat. He was then marched back to Hillsborough and discharged after he had served five months.
2. George Nease (Neese) #R7570 – served under Capt. John Clendenin and with said captain was made prisoner in Hillsboro….when that town was taken by certain Tories under the command of Col Fanning and that this applicant with other prisoners then and there made was taken to Wilmington…confined on board a British brig for some weeks as prisoners of war, from thence were conveyed to Charleston and there put on board of a British prison ship called the "ESKE" and there was closely imprisoned till some time (he thinks) in July when he was regularly exchanged being as correctly as he can compute eleven months…
3. David Blalock #S3011 – My last period of service was 3 month tour; I was drafted in the state troops at Pittsboro and rendezvous at Ramsey Mill. The first excursion was to meet Col. Fanning. News arrived at about midnight that the Colonel had plundered Hillsboro and was making his way for the east now. That he would be at Cane creek better known by the name of Lindley Creek soon. We had a desperate encounter for a few moments, they were said to be 6 or 800 strong, we were much less numerous than they – we were commanded by Gen Butler, Col Nall and Luttrell, my captain was Ma (damaged) Jones and Lieu Rob Jones a brother. We met them about one hour by sun on the morning. We attempted to stop their passage by the creek side. They made a desperate charge upon us Col Nall and Luttrell and my captain in the first tour of 3 mths fell….The death of our officers insured our defeat, but the Tory Col made no halt to bury the dead but passed right off. In counting the dead were found we had lost fifty and had killed 15 Tories. We buried the dead on the creek side, putting all the Tories into one pit and marched back to the barracks…."
4. John Woods #S1887 "He states that Col Fanning of the Tories came to Hillsboro and plundered the town with a band of Tories and took the most of the citizens of orange county prisoners and marched them all down to Lindley's mill. He states that the citizens of orange county in the neighborhood of Hillsboro collected together and marched on in order to rescue the prisoner taken at Hillsborough and met with Col Butler and Col Maybe and on that tour which was only about 1 week and a small engagement or skirmish with the Tories near Lindley's Mill, but was not able to retake our prisoners.
5. Gatus Fox #R3725 Served under Lytle they marched to Hillsboro and stationed there to guard the place it being the residence of the governor. After having remained at the station for a short time, perhaps a month, they were attacked by Fanning by whom they were defeated and all made prisoner including the Governor. They were carried to Wilmington where they were kept in a prison in a place called the "Provo's". While here the small pox broke out among them and many of them died of that disease. After remaining in this place for about 3 months was exchanged.
6. Benjamin Austin #S6548 Vol 6 mths under Capt Abraham Allen under the command of Col Hugh Teenan. He was taken prisoner Sep 12 by the Tories that took Gov Burke, taken to Wilmington place on board a prison ship and sent to Charleston, from thence to Johns Island new Charleston where he remained some time and thence to Savannah GA from which he made his escape from the enemy on the night of the 9th of April 1782 and went up the savannah river where Gen Wayne was stationed.
7. Edward Almond (Allman) #S6489 – He knows of his first tour of 3 mths as he himself served with him under Col Luttrell and as to his 2nd service he was a prisoner under the Tories as the time of the battle of Lindley's mills where his brother was a solider in the service.
8. James Allison #S6491 – The day after the Tories took Hillsboro he vol in the County of Orange in the light horse commanded by Capt. Thompson and pursued the Tories to the neighborhood of Wilmington. In the vicinity of Wilmington at a place called the raft swamp we attacked under Butler and Mebane and routed them. The declarent was in the battle.
9. Thomas Miles #R7168 – 2nd tour as a vol mounted man began Sep 1, 1781 under Gen Butler, volunteers rendezvoused at Hillsboro thence marched to Fayetteville, then to near Wilmington to with the movements of Maj Craig and Fanning. In this tour the applicant was under the command of Gen Butler, Col Moore, Capt Spillby Coleman, Lieu James Burton where his company commanders, during which an engagement

took place at Baldwin's plantation (Brown Marsh), the combat was at night, the Americans retained possession of the ground. (NOTE: there are 2 - Thomas Miles in the pension files - #14 below)

10. John Mebane #S9403 – prisoner, marched to Wilmington and thrown unto a prison ship where he remained for several weeks then he was paroled. **James Turner** a witness for the application stated "the town was taken by the Tories and that presently after being his prisoners they were all for a short time confined in the Hillsboro jail for safe keeping till the Tory party had plundered the town and he well remembers that said John Mebane was brought into the jail he danced across the floor and that upon the Tory parties leaving Hillsboro all the prisoners they then and there made, were place under guard and speedily marched to Wilmington. Confined on British ship for 2 weeks said John Mebane was paroled while this affiant and other prisoners were carried to Charleston and sometime in 1782 were released.
11. Richard Christmas #S8196 – Volunteer 7/15/1781 was capt on parole when he joined again and was taken a prisoner under Fanning, taken to Charleston on board prison ship ESKE and was exchanged July 1782. - *** James Turner back as a witness again – said he was under the command of Capt Clendenin. And was released April 1782 on the ESKE as well.
12. Matthew McCauley #W17121 – wife said that her husband was prisoner with Lytle and Mebane. Her husband was Captain of Orange County militia. "This declarant remembers the capture of Hillsboro very well, as it was so distressing to her husband as captain was taken by the said Tory forces to Wilmington then by sea to Charleston and to the ship ESKE." "She remembers the name of the vessel very well, as she has frequently heard her husband speak of the hardships he suffered on board of said prison ship. She said he was release either the first day of March or April of 1782. Col O'Neal and Gen Butler were his superiors.
13. Massey Medaris (McDavis) #S9410 – entered the service under Gen Butler and Capt Clark, after the battle of Guilford. From Chatham court house he was marched to Crow's Ford on Haw River. The Tories but a short time before had taken the town of Hillsboro from which place they retired to Lindley Mill on Cane Creek. About 2 hours before day, this declarent marched with 250 volunteers with him to Crow's ford to attack the Tories on Cane Creek. Tories numbered of 700 were defeated with loss of 100 men and completely dispersed. The loss of the Whigs being only 17. The success of this campaign was due to Mebane. He also fought at Brown Marsh.
14. Thomas Miles #W8457 – He together with Capt. Foley made up a volunteer company of 48 men and march after the Tories to Hillsboro and went on pursuit and overhauled them at Lindleys mill, where they had a very severe fought with them. Lutterrel died, together with many others. There were most of the Tories killed. Joined Rutherford and fought again.
15. Joseph Neely #S31879 – Capt Nells and Mebane, took Lytle and some of the citizens of the town prisoners. Mebane was in command of the light horse, this declerant one of them, "was stationed between the mill and the enemy in order to fall in on the rear. Fanning marched to the mill and was fired on by Butler which was returned by Fanning where Butler retreated then Mebane attacked them in the rear and after a considerable skirmish Mebane kept the ground to the loss of Fanning being 30 killed and wounded, Col Mebane had but about 75 men after the battle. Butler was not seen that day again.
16. Holloway Pass #S7289 – Volunteered under Capt Adam Sanders in Caswell Co and met up with Col William Moore and Maj Dudley Renolds and they to Fayetteville in pursuit of Tories and prisoners and joined up with Gen Butler at a place called Brown Marsh and had a severe engagement and was defeated by bad management of Gen Butler and if it had not been for old Col Mebane of Orange Regiment we would have been all taken prisoners. From this place we retreated to Cross Creek (Fayetteville).
17. Henry Albright #S6485 – Joined under Capt Trousdale and Lieu John Campbell and they were stationed in Hillsboro. He was appointed Sgt, and after a few weeks and the Tories captured the town and Governor and many of his men and taken to Wilmington and then onto a British ship and then the ship went to Charleston and remained there for 11 months and then exchanged July 1782 and arrived home August 6.
18. Ludwick Albright #W5609 – he served under Maj O'Neal and Gen Butler and served with Robert Mebane at Lindley Mill.
19. William Allen #S30822 – under John Campbell and Robert Scoby and then under Col Lytle and Fanning took about 300 people. He saw Col Lytle get wounded in the head by Fanning. "That night we remained near Hillsborough and were carried by the British next morning to a place called Lindley's Mill were a pretty severe and well fought battle took place..."He recollects seeing Tory McNeil killed. That night they took off to a place called Wilson's Iron Work then to Wilmington and then on a ship. The ship was to go to the West Indies but landed in Charleston and remained there until paroled in August 11, 1782.
20. Isaac Brewer #R1185 – Served with Nalls and Mebane. He fought at Lindley's Mill and said Fanning supposedly had 900 men and Mebane 4-500. The deponent states that the action continued about one hour

and the conflict was a sharp one. Mebane ordered a retreat and the deponent was shot in the back near the spine and has never been retracted. During the action at Lindley Nalls and McNeil died and "A good many men were killed and wounded on both sides."

21. John Brownlow - #R1358 – Served under Capt Joseph Rosser and Col Robert Mebane, he was in the vanguard at Lindley mill was wounded and left for dead. He was wounded in three places in the skull which was broken with a sword by one of the enemy. He laid at his mothers in Chatham County for many months recovering. "In the said battle I received four wounds three of them on my head all of which broke the skull and 13 pieces of the skull bone larger and smaller were taken from one of the said wounds on my head – the other wound was on my wrist of my left arm." He never received any compensation for his service!!!!!
22. John Copeland #R2310 – Joined Chatham County to pursue Fanning. He fought under John Nalls who died and 14 soldiers.
23. David Higdon #W25769 – under Maj Galston and Mebane and fought at Lindley Mill in which the Tories were defeated and Hector O'Neil was killed along with several others. Some were slain on the Whig side of which he knew - Billy Dillard.
24. William Nichols #?????? – Fought at Lindley mill – "We got in the bushes of a long hill about 50 yards from the road, we fired on them and completely routed and defeated and killed their commander McNeil, took a good many prisoners and retook the Governor. Butler and Mebane were in command.
25. Benjamin Standifer #??????? – Fought at Lindley's Mill – no real details.
26. Isaac Brewer - #?????? – Joined under Mebane and Capt Bill Smith and was in Hillsboro. Mebane had 4-500 men, Tories had over 900 and the battle lasted some 3 or 4 hours, and the Tories were commanded by old Hector McNeil and David Fanning. They ultimately proved too hard for our men and were slaying our ranks down by the scores. Mebane thought it best to retreat instead of being taken and did so. The result of which was that they mowed us down more rapidly than before. In carrying out the order, Isaac was shot in the back.
27. James Kell #S32357 – Elected Captain of a militia company in orange county and fought at Lindley's Mill and then marched with Mebane and Butler to Cross Creek.
28. John Searcy #S31355 he was detained as a prisoner with the governor and a "few others" and taken to Wilmington and then on to a British ship.
29. William Slade #W4069 – Col Moore and Dudley Renolds were marched to Fayetteville to a place called white marsh (I assume Brown Marsh) where we overtook them and made an attack, but were compelled to retreat and were marched from place to place back to Fayetteville.
30. Andrew Harwell #S31104 – Enlisted under Capt White to go to Wilmington and retake the Governor, but we were unsuccessful and were defeated.
31. Thomas Hargis #S8663 – Joined for 3 months after hearing about the Gov being captured and served under Capt Shadrach Hargis. Also under Gen Butler and Col Moore. We had a skirmish near Wilmington and in that engagement Gen Butlers horse ran off with the General as it was rumored – but this declarant then though and still thinks that it was the General and not the horse that was the author of the blunder. Out of about 500 American nearly 300 retreated before the Enemy, with Gen Butler and his horse and after the falling back of the Americans, the declarant shot several guns believe that if he again should fall into the hands of the enemy, that death would inevitably be his fate.
32. Samuel Shepherd #S21476 – His captain was Mark Patterson and General Marmady. His brother was killed in the battle at Lindley's Mill, but he was not present. He was present at the skirmish at Coxes Mill on the deep river and short time after Lindley.
33. George Baker #S2953 – Joined under Col Moore from Caswell Co and Capt John Oldham and marched after the battle at Lindley's and joined forces with Gen Butler at Brown March and had a "warm skirmish" with them. Then marched to Fayetteville and joined Rutherford.
34. Lewis Bledsoe #W17315 – fought at Lindley's mill, "held the ground" then back to Hillsborough ad then with reinforcements went to Brown Marsh and fought there and then on to Fayetteville.
35. Rich Jacob #W26380 - The town of Hillsboro was attacked by the enemy our company was encamped about one mile therefrom. We marched hastily to the relief of the place and then became engaged with the enemy who had a superior force. Our company was all killed or taken prisoners except five." He also said "In the summer of 1781 there was a number of prisoners of war confined in jail at Hillsboro. At that time I was in the service as a Lieu in the company of Capt. John Clendenin who was a Continental officer, had been taken prisoner ??????? (cant make it out) South Carolina, was paroled, returned home, broke his parole and raised a company of volunteers.."

36. Benjamin Grist #W1170 – He was at the battle of the Catawba N.C. under Capt. Clendenin and Col Belford – At the battle at Lindley's Mill under the same officers where he was wounded in his head, his skull broke, was in the skirmishes at …
37. Buckner Smith #W1325 – He enlisted under Capt. John Clendenin of Col Arch Little [Lytle] regiment N.C. line and was with Gen Greene at the battle of Guilford and was also at the Battle at Lindley's Mill where he was wounded in four places, his body, head, thigh and hand and has now the scars to witness it. He was also at the Battle of Hanging Rock….
38. Robert Burnside #S17304 – he volunteered with Capt John Clendenin – said to be a of the regular dragoons that we marched through Orange county N.C. to the relief of Hillsborough which we found in the hands of a Col McNeil commandant of the Tories our Captain pushed into the town where we were fired upon and after completed to give way this applicant was thrown by his horse and taken prisoner and put in jail but broke from there the same night and returned home.
39. Elijah Fooshee (R3635) – "we marched out to hunt them, which we did about the middle of march at Lindley's mill on Cain Creek on the road to Hillsboro – we had our whole force about 80 in number and Col. Luttrell was in command the Tories were commanded by Col Fanning a celebrated Scotch Tory and the same Captain Duck before named with about 120 men. The battle commenced about 9 o'clock and continued about one hour when the Tories retreated having about 36 killed on the field Captain Duck being among the slain. Col Fanning as we understood afterwards was wounded in the action but made his escape. On our side there were four killed and three wounded. Col Luttrell while gallantly fighting at the head of the Regiment was killed. The Tories were mounted and our troops were on foot and consequently did not pursue them. This was about 6 miles from our station to which we returned after the action with the corpse of our beloved Colonel after having buried the other three gallant fellows in coffins on the battleground.

(Picture from the battle area on the patriot side. This image was taken with the photographer's back where the Tories were crossing. Could a patriot have used this rock to shoot from?)

Here is an alphabetical list of the pensions found with the Lindley Mill event.

Last Name	First	Location	Who was in command & Misc notes
Albright	Ludwick	Lindley Mill	Col Mebane
Albright	Henry	Prisoner	Capt James Trousdale, Lieu John Campbell - prison ship abt 11mnths - July 1782
Allen	William	Prisoner	Archibald Lytle, exchanged 8/11/1782 - on a ship
Allison	James	Lindley Mill	Col Mebane, volunteered Capt. Thompson "light horse" for Orange County
Allman	Nathan	Lindley Mill	Served under Luttrell (fought to free brother)
Allman	Edward	Prisoner	Gave no information
Austin	Benjamin	Prisoner	Capt. Abraham Allen, Col Hugh Teenan, escaped during transfer of prisons Apr 9, 1782
Barker	George	Brown Marsh	Col. William Moore, Capt John Odham - took place about midnight
Barker	David	Brown Marsh	Caswell Co, under Cap. Oldham and Col Moore, British Troops and Tories Brown Marsh
Blalock	David	Lindley Mill	Gen Butler, Col Nalls, Col Littrell, Lieu Rob Jones
Bledsoe	Lewis	Brown Marsh	with reinforcements fought at a place called Brown Marsh.
Bledsoe	Lewis	Lindley Mill	fought at Lindley's Mill - held our ground - returned to Hillsborough
Brener	Isaac	Lindley Mill	Capt. William Smith, John Nalls, Robert Mebane, provided details of battle
Brewer	Isaac	Lindley Mill	Supposed to be 900 Tories, we supposed to have 4-500 lasted 1 hour, Brewer wounded
Browning	Robert	Brown Marsh	Butler ordered retreat due to artillary, and there wasn't any
Brownlow	John	Lindley Mill	Capt Joseph Russer, Col Mebane, wounded left for dead 13-pieces of skull bone
Burnside	Robert	Hillsboro	Capt. John Clenddin captured at Hillsboro, put in the jail, he escaped from the jail
Christmas	Richard	Prisoner	Prison ship Eske, exch for Capt. Osbourn July 1, 1782
Clark	James	Lindley Mill	fought with Col Mebane and Gen Butler - said 77 horses strong
Collins	Eli	Lindley Mill	Attached Fanning at Lindley's Mill
Collins	Eli	Brown Marsh	They had another skirmish near Wimington with the Tories and British
Copeland	John	Lindley Mill	Served under Nells - said 14 died
Draffon	John	Lindley Mill	Capt Cage at Luttrells Barracks, fought at Lindley's Mill
Earthman	Isaac	Lindley Mill	Capt Gwinn, sent to watch the Tories leaving Hillsboro, fought at Lindley - Fanning killed
Edwards	Robert	Lindley Mill	Under Gen Butler and Col Mebane, doesn't remember his Capt.
Elkins	Joshua	Lindley Mill	Under Capt McCullers
Fooshee	Elijah	Lindley Mill	we had 80, commenced at 9am, Capt Duck killed, continued about 1 hour
Forrest	James	Lindley Mill	two parties fought at Lindleys, Whigs were overpowered compelled to retreat
Forrest	James	Brown Marsh	Butler collected with reinforcements not able to overtake due to large British force
Fox	Gatus	Prisoner	Lytle, prisoner for 3 mths, sent to prison - "Provo"
Geane	Phillip	Lindley Mill	Pension states that he was one of those **killed at the battle**
Greeen	William	Lindley Mill	counted 31 dead on the ground besides others near the mill, Luttrell died later
Greeen	William	Brown Marsh	Reached Livingstons Bridge about 300 enemy, lasted 15 minutes, retreated
Gregory	William	Lindley Mill	joined Capt Alexander Clark, joined Ben Gbutlers met Tories at Lindley's Mill
Grist	Benjamin	Lindley Mill	Capt. Clendennen & Col Belford - he was wounded in the head at the battle Lindley Mill
Hargis	Thomas	Brown Marsh	Capt Shadrach Hargis, Gen Butler, somewere near Wilm. He said Butler fled the battle
Harwell	Andrew	Brown Marsh	Capt White and Gen Butler, mentioned they retreated
Higdon	Daniel	Lindley Mill	said he knew that his friend Billy Dillard was killed
Howell	Benjamin	Lindley Mill	Col Luttrell and Maj Nalls killed - we whipped them, drove them to Raft Swamp
Ivy	Henry	Lindley Mill	fought at Lindley Mill with a part of toried under Col Fanning.
Johnson	Robert	Lindley Mill	killed 36 Tories
Kell	James	Lindley Mill	Col Mebane
Manis	Seth	Lindley Mill	sharp action, he retreated and we dod not take him nor any of his men
Marler	Joseph	Lindley Mill	had a skirmish with the Tories near a place called Lindley's Mill in which Tories defeated
Matthews	John	Prisoner	He said that he was captured "on their way" and McKay parolled him before Wilmington
McCauley	Matthew	Prisoner	Lieu Archibald Lytle - 6 months on Eske
McDavis	Massey	Lindley Mill	Gen Butler, Capt Clark - he gave details of battle
McElroy	John	Lindley Mill	Capt. Lewis Bledsoe originally under Capt. McCuller's Company
McElroy	Micajah	Lindley Mill	Col Mebane in charge, fought tories
Meachem	Richard	Lindley Mill	9 miles from Luttrell's, I was wounded in the hip, 37 scotts and 26 tories, 4 patriots killed
Meares	Joel	Lindley Mill	Marched against Fanning and McNeil who commanded 700 Tories
Mebane	John	Prisoner	Prison Ship for several weeks exch for Lieu McClain
Miles	Thomas	Lindley Mill	Capt Foley and his 48 volunteers from Chatham Co. some details given
Miles (#2)	Thomas	Brown Marsh	Gen Butler, Col Moore, Capt Spillsby Coleman, Lieu James Burton
Mitchell	William	Lindley Mill	Col Maben, were some 30 or 40 tories killed and several of our little force
Mitchell	William	Brown Marsh	crossed river at Browns Ferry, Fanning rec. 300 British under Maj Craig we had 150-200
Mitchell	Jesse	Lindley Mill	Lieu Abraham Bryant, Jacob Duck, Robert Maybin, skirmish at Lindley's Mill
Moore	Henry	Lindley Mill	under Capt McFarland, 5 men were killed, Col Luttrell and 7 wounded, killed several Tory
Moore	James	Lindley Mill	McDouglad (tory) killed, Nalls killed - there were 250 prisoners from Hillsboro
Myrick	Moses	Lindley Mill	Under Capt. Jacob Duck, rendezvoused at Maj Nall residence, then fought at Lindley
Neely	Joseph	Lindley Mill	Capt Nells, Col Mebane - gave details
Neese	George	Prisoner	Capt John Clendenin, Wilmington to Eske to Charleston - July 1782 release
Nichols	William	Lindley Mill	he said they won, took prisoners! Said they fought along the side of a long hill
Parrish	Claiborne	Lindley Mill	Party of tories took prisoners-we intercepted at Lindley's Mill where we had engagement
Pass	Holloway	Brown Marsh	Capt. Adam Sanders, Col William Moore, Col Dudley Reynolds - details
Pearson	Paris	Lindley Mill	application filed by his wife, said he was in a horse company under Butler
Poplin	George	Lindley Mill	Under Maj Nalls, battle lasted 3 hours, Col Goldston, Mebane in command
Ragains	Thomas	Lindley Mill	routed them, took 25 prisoners to Mr. Lindley's house
Ray	Francis	Brown Marsh	Under Capt. Adam Sanders, Gov captured, pursued to Brown Marsh, we were defeated
Ray	William	Lindley Mill	Captain of Orange Co. Militia under Mebane and Butler, fought at Lindley's Mill
Rich	Jacob	Hillsboro	he was wounded by Fanning as they entered Hillsboro - he survived
Shepard	Samuel	Coxes Mill	Capt Mark Peterson, Gen Francis Malmady
Slade	William	White Marsh	Capt Adam Sander, Lieu M. Lea, Col. William Moore, Maj Dudley Reynolds
Smith	Buckner	Lindley Mill	Capt. Clendennen under Col Lytle fought at Lindley's Mill, 4 wounds, scars remain
Smith	William	Lindley Mill	Changed a few rounds, told they would kill prisoners, we waited to see where they went
Smith	William	Brown Marsh	Arrived at a swamp, sent 16 spies to find the tories, were captured, but esc during fight
Standifer	Benjamin	Lindley Mill	he knew that Luttrell and Nells died
Stevens	Moab	Brown Marsh	Gen Butler and Col Robeson - British and Tories under the command of Major Craig
Stroud	Matthew	Lindley Mill	difficult to read - Mentions Nells and Butler
Thrash	Valentine	Brown Marsh	Col Moore, small engagement with British and Tories at a place called Brown Marsh
Turner	James	Prisoner	Taken across Woody's Ferry, then to Stallworth, then Lindley's, then on Eske
Williams	David	Lindley Mill	under Col Taylor, 200 Patriots, 30-40 Tory killed, Tories had 406 men
Williams	David	Brown Marsh	400 men, Brown's Ferry, Col Moore had 4-500 men, Livingston Swamp, Craig had 300
Wood	John	Lindley Mill	took most of the citizens of Orange County prisoner, fought at Lindley's Mill

Appendix B - Thomas Hart – Jesse Benton

Thomas Hart was a citizen of Hillsborough from the early 1760's. He fought against the Regulators during that war (May 1771). This is how he received the title "Colonel", as he sometimes referred. Thomas was a wealthy, and influential citizen of Orange County. He bought the Maddox Mill when Maddox left Hillsborough as he realized Gov Tryon and Edmund Fanning were soon to clash with the Regulators. Some historians say that Maddox was told to leave, as his mill site was the meeting location for the Regulators. Never the less, Thomas Hart expands the mill site into a complex, soon to be called - Hartford. A long and complex story shortened, Thomas Hart leaves Hillsborough to Hagerstown, MD, and Jesse Benton ultimately takes care of Hartford, as well as Hart's business debts, and ventures.

Jesse Benton wrote Thomas many times, with some lengthy letters. These amazingly detailed letters ultimately made their way to one of Thomas Hart's daughters, husband, Henry Clay, and this in turn resides in the Library of Congress in the Manuscript division. Usually these letters are quoted in part, sometimes just a line, and others are paraphrased. Copies were purchased of every letter, and then transcribed. (See the Reference section of this book for details) Jesse Benton was a lawyer, and his letters include personal notes about the citizens, agriculture issues, currency difficulties, debates on Americas future, and just a great view of life after the Revolutionary War, until his untimely death in the 1790's.

I think his letter about the Fanning/Lindley Mill situation is so important since he was a citizen in Hillsborough, and he wrote this letter soon after the attack on the town. This is just as valuable as Iredell's letter, due to being written soon thereafter, not a historical remembrance. Sometimes as stories are handed down through the generations, they get altered or missing details are embellished. None of these letters produce the details we all would like to know, but in weighing their accuracy, they should be put in front of family stories, and passed down traditions.

(Note: Letter is from the Library of Congress, Manuscript Department, Henry Clay Papers, September 29, 1781 – Jesse Benton to Thomas Hart)

Enoe, 29th of September 1781

Dear Colonel,
Yours of the 4th of August by Mr. Porterfield I received a few days ago and shall endeavor to comply with the contents as soon as time & opportunity [missing] allow me : I have not yet understood wh[missing] Kellow nor his attorney Mr. Holland are [missing] however, am told that Mr. Kellow was at Ge[missing] two weeks ago.

If I am not misinformed [missing] of the stills which you sold Kellow, is taken away by Robert Dickins, & the other together with a set of Smith tools, were attached last Spring at the instance of one Mr. Newman. I've not seen Robert Nelson since the receipt of your letter. I think a wagon may easily be hired to go in with the stills provided they can be got together in time.

You will receive enclosed a letter from Mr. Brame, in consequence of which, I sent him a copy of the bill of sale & informed him that you have the bond. Mr. Mallett remains with the British in Wilmington, & comes within the meaning of the Governor's Proclamation for confiscating the property [missing] Tories, & other who have failed to come out [missing] General Exchange of prisoners.

I am very glad you got away from here [missing] time you did; for had you remained, [missing] convinced your moveable property would have been plundered from you, & yourself a prisoner, as had lately been the case with a great number of our best men. Our state has really become odious, owing (I am afraid) to mismanagement in the Legislative or Executive powers a small party of British, not exceeding 400, have been in Wilmington ever since last winter, have had free communication with the Tories in the country, & meeting with no opposition have made them so formidable that the state is next to being reduced. One David Fanning (an old horse thief) & Hector McNeil have kidnapped almost every leading man between here & Wilmington. The last stroke they made was the 12th of this month when they came into Hillsborough at 7 O'Clock in the morning with 500 Tories killed five or six of the guard, took the Governor, several gentlemen, the inhabitants of the Town, Continentals & Militia troops, amounting in the whole to 140 odd men; made a general Jail delivery by setting at liberty about 40, Criminal, Deserters & Delinquents, whom they armed with our public muskets, & have since carried the prisoners safe into Wilmington, all except about a dozen who got paroled & escaped on the way. This said Fanning & McNeil had hovered about the Buffalo Ford on Deep River two or three weeks preceding this accident with their men embodied; Gen Butler & Col Robert Mebane with 200 horse & 100 Foot had been 5 or 6 days near Crows Ford on Haw River to watch their motions however the Tories executed their designs. About 100 of the neighbors under the command of Col Thomas Taylor pursued the Tories the evening of the 12th instant (myself in company) with a resolution to surprise their camp by night, but were so unfortunate as not to find the main body until after sunrise, tho, we passed them six miles and followed a party of about 100 (which were not the object of our attention at the time.) When we discovered the main camp near James Tinnen's we were in imminent danger, & retreated to Hillsborough where we got reinforced, foraged & pursued again. In the course of the night we dispatched three men to find Gen Butler which they effected a little before day & gave him the first account of what has happened. He then threw himself in the Enemys Road below Doctor Pile's & marched up to Lindley's Mill where he met the Tories, engaged them immediately & gave them a total defeat, tho' the prisoners were carried off by them. Upwards of fifty Tories killed; Col Luterell, Major Nalls & six privates on our side killed. Col Hector McNeil, Capt Doud, one M. Cloud & several men in officers garb among the Tories were left dead. The Highlanders ventured with only Broadsword & Dirks so near that they received both powder & ball at the same time & fell like heroes indeed. Capt Abrm Allen with 50 men had a battle lately with Dick

Edwards & his Company killed Edwards & 4 or 5 more. Allen got shot through the body tho' will get well, Lt Joseph Young & 2 privates killed on our side. The militia of the state has at last got in motion, Wilmington is the object. This is all the news I can at present recollect; so I conclude dear Col, with my wife's compliments joins me with my own, to Mrs. Hart, Miss Betsey, Col Rochester & yourself.

    Your most Obt Serv.

    Jesse Benton

P.S. Gen Greene has certainly cut the British Army in the southward, to pieces; some say 300 escaped, others say Lee & Marion took them. I don't know [missing] Col Rochester [missing] some of your papers; I looked slightly [missing] & Sam. Chamber's notes & did not [missing].

Appendix C – Lindley History

The location of this historical site is in southeast Alamance County, today. In the 1780's it was in southwest Orange County. In 1849, Alamance County was formed from Orange.

The earliest image that we can see of the area comes from the 1938 aerial photographs. These images, were stitched together and enhanced in order to increase detail. The image below is cropped to show specific details of the battle ground area, and the mill.

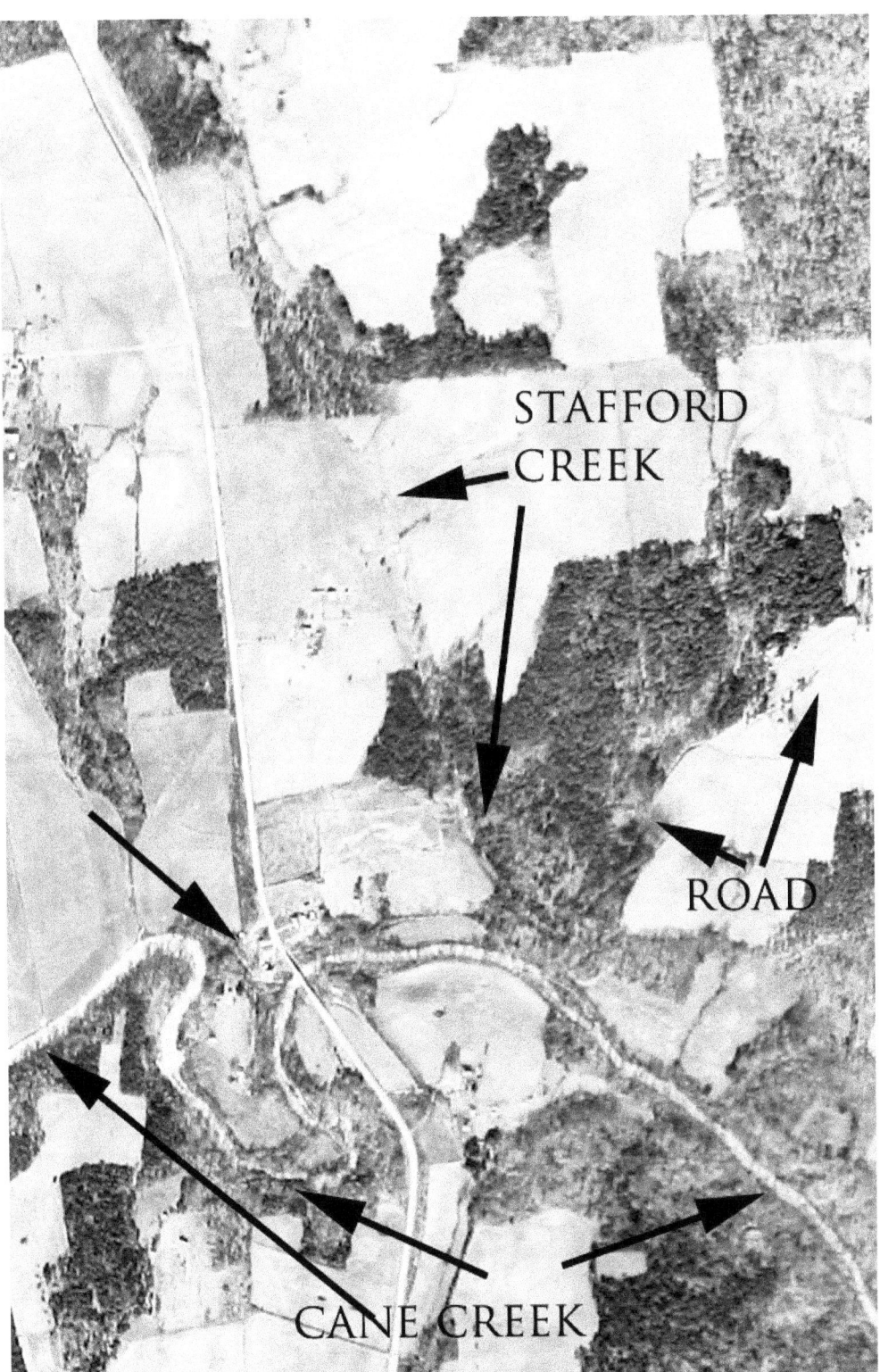

Here is a stitched together image, showing a larger perspective.

Cropped image of the 1938 aerial. North is straight-up.

Amazingly, this area has not been that altered, as the battle location remains – untouched! This is a 2005 GIS image.

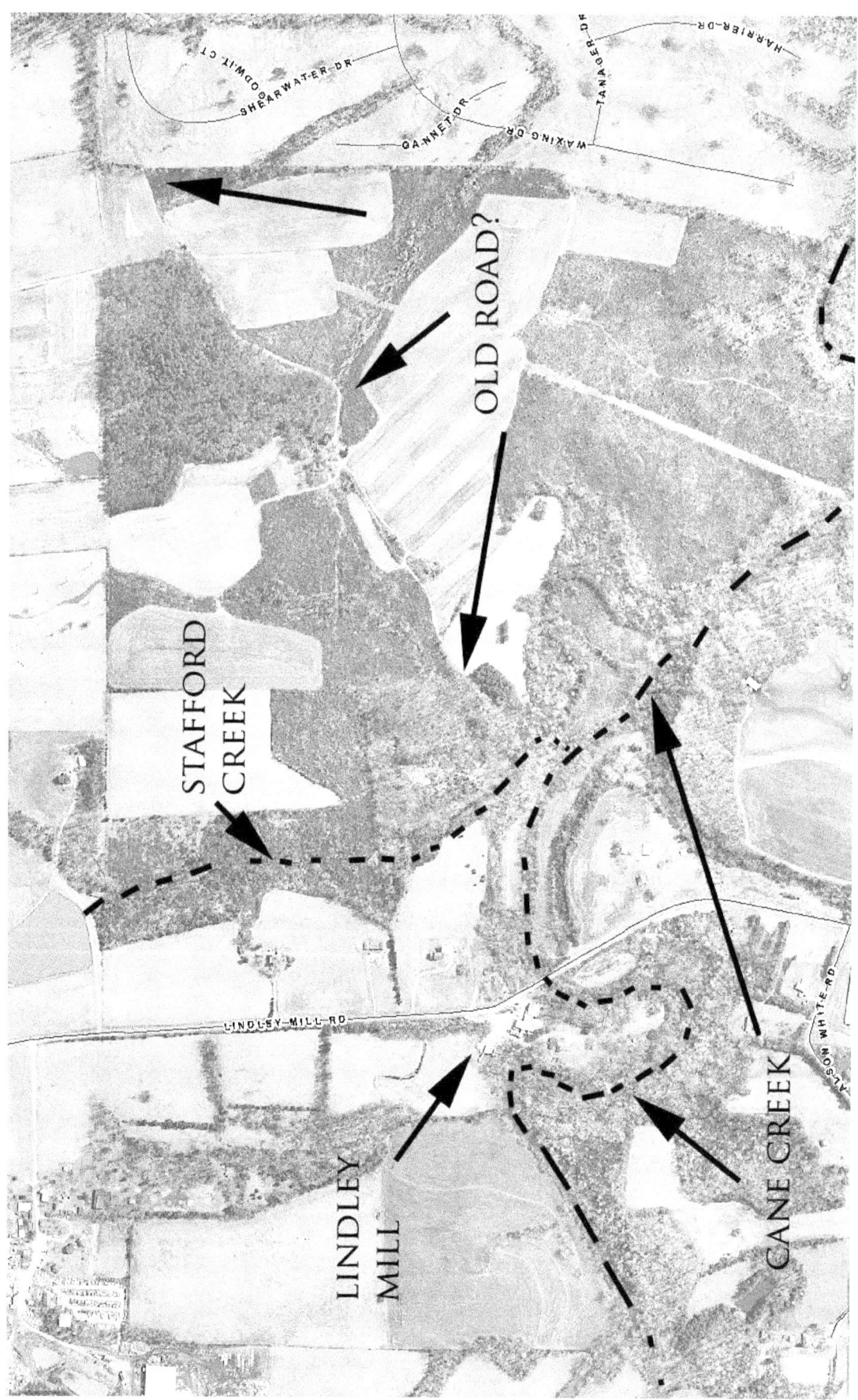

Here is a copy of the Spoon Map (1893) of Alamance County. This shows the general area in discussion.

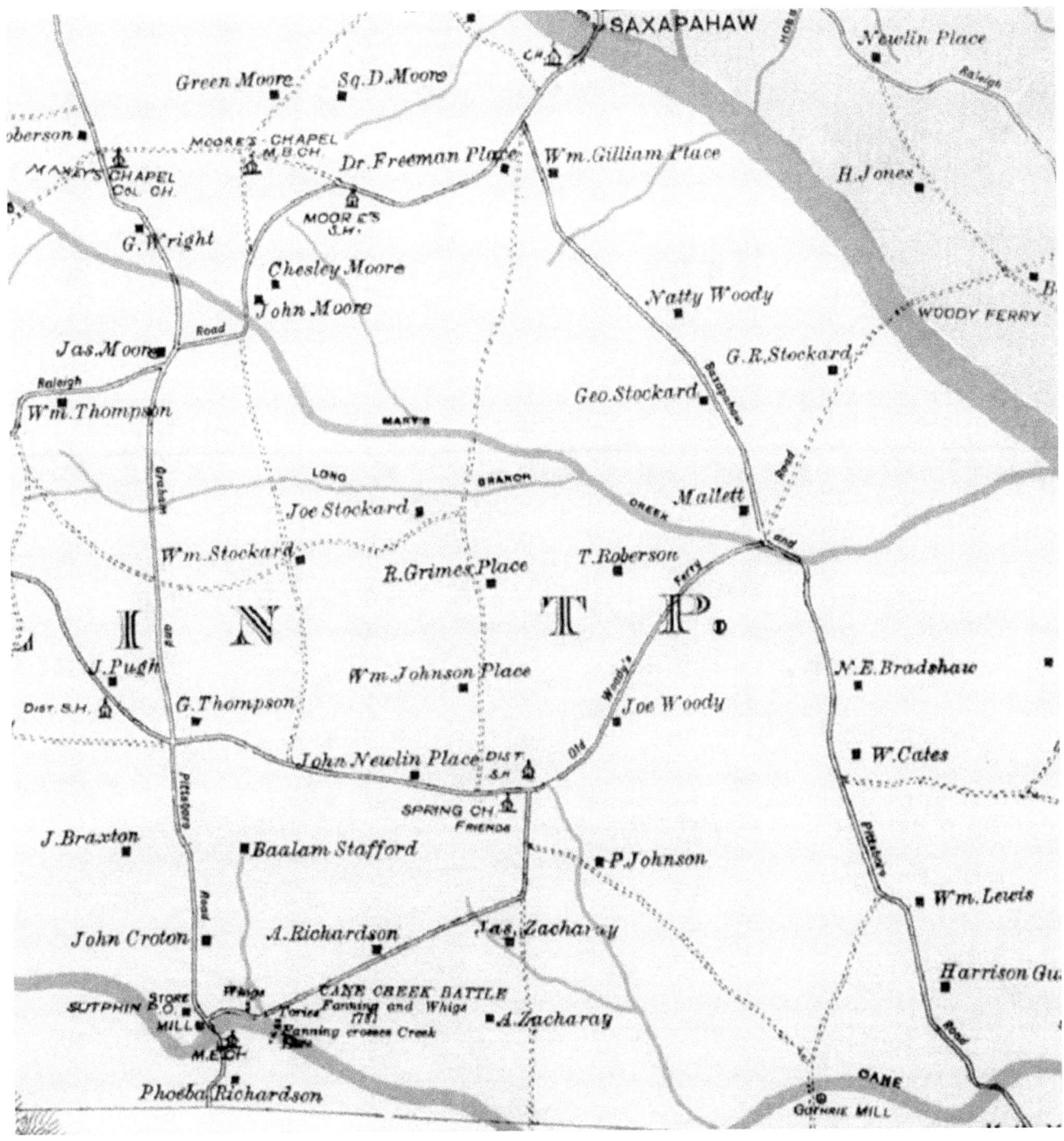

Cropped image of the Spoon map showing the Mill area and battlefield location.

Lindley Family Overview

I don't want to turn this book into a genealogy book, nor a family reference book. However, it might help the reader in understanding the division of sentiment between remaining loyal and not. Lastly, to follow the mill's history, you will need to know some of the family members (they used the name Thomas many times, for many generations).

Thomas Lindley and his wife Ruth Hadley are from Pennsylvania and move to North Carolina in the 1750's. They have many children, of which those that survive infancy, are as follows:

- Catherine (b. 9/22/1732, m. 10/21/1731, d. 5/1/1811) Married William White.
- James (b. 9/22/1735, d.2/14/1779) – Tory officer at Battle of Kettle Creek, hanged.
- Thomas Jr. (b. 8/7/1740, m. 12/13/1790, d. 2/28/1833) Married Sarah Evans.
- William (b. 12/27/1742/3, m. abt. 1764, d. 9/29/1784) Married Mary Morton (Tory – killed)
- Ruth (b. 3/25/1745, m. , d. 7/15/1798) Married Joshua Hadley
- John (b. 10/13/1747, m.3/16/1768, d. 7/5/1798) Married Sarah Pyle, Tory officer under D. Fanning
- Eleanor (b. 9/15/1750, m.4/18/1767, d.1/12/1783) Married Geo. Harris
- Jonathan (b.6/15/1756, m. , d.4/5/1828) Married Deborah Dicks

Descendants of James Lindley

1 James Lindley 1681 - 1726
.. +Eleanor Parke 1683/84 -
.... 2 Thomas Lindley 1705/06 - 1781
.... +Ruth Hadley 1711 -
.... 3 Catherine Lindley 1732 -
.... 3 James Lindley 1735 - 1779
.... 3 Simon Lindley 1737/38 -
.... 3 Thomas Lindley 1740 - 1833
.... +Sarah Evans 1743 -
.... 4 Owen Lindley 1763 -
.... 4 William Lindley 1764 -
.... 4 Thomas Lindley 1766 -
.... 4 Aaron Lindley 1768 -
.... 4 Jonathan Lindley 1770 -
.... 4 David Lindley 1771 -
.... 4 James Lindley 1774 -
.... 4 Mary Lindley 1775 -
.... 4 Joshua Lindley 1778 -
.... 4 John Lindley 1780 -
.... 4 Sarah Lindley 1782 -
.... 3 William Lindley 1742 - 1784
.... +Mary Morton 1738 -
.... 4 Ruth Lindley 1765 -
.... +Jehu Pyle 1766 -
.... 4 Samuel Lindley 1769 -
.... +Mary Braxton 1776 - 1846
.... 5 Mary Lindley 1802 -
.... 5 Ann Lindley 1807 -
.... 4 Mary Lindley 1774 -
.... 4 Elizabeth Lindley 1776 - 1778
.... 4 William Lindley 1779 -
.... 4 Thomas Lindley 1769 - 1825
.... +Jane Hoopes 1778 -
.... 5 William Lindley 1796 -
.... 5 Deborah Lindley 1811 -
.... 5 Mary Lindley 1797 -
.... 5 Samuel Lindley
.... 5 Abraham Lindley 1801 -
.... 5 Hannah Lindley 1814 -
.... 5 John Hoopes Lindley 1816 -
.... 3 Ruth Lindley 1745 -
.... 3 Eleanor Lindley 1750 - 1783
.... 4 Mary Lindley Chambers
.... 3 Deborah Lindley 1753 -
.... +James Newlin 1747 - 1813
.... 3 Jonathan Lindley 1756 - 1828
.... +Deborah Dicks 1756 -
.... 4 Zachariah Lindley 1776 -
.... 4 Hannah Lindley 1780 -
.... 4 Thomas Lindley 1782 -
.... 4 Eleanor Lindley 1784 -
.... 4 William Lindley 1787 -
.... 4 deborah Lindley 1789 -
.... 4 Mary Lindley 1792 -
.... 4 Catherine Lindley 1794 -
.... 4 Sarah Lindley 1786 -
.... 4 Jonathan Lindley 1800 -
.... 3 Mary Lindley 1758 -
.... 3 John Lindley 1474 - 1798
.... +Sarah Pyle 1750 -
.... 4 Samuel Washington Lindley 1788 -
.... 4 Jonathan Lindley

Here is a general time-period overview of the Lindley family activities.

1750-1780

During this time, the Lindley's continue to have children, with their youngest and last child (son), Jonathan (1756). Thomas and Hugh Laughlin created a partnership and built a mill for the local area. This would be for southwest Orange County and part of (soon to be created) Chatham County. This early mill will be shown on both the Collett and Mouzon maps (1770 and 1775). The highway from Hillsborough runs southwest towards one of a number of river crossings on the Haw River. In particular, there is a branch of the road that runs more south-southwest towards a famous and well documented – Woody's Ferry. The road continues on the western side of the Haw River proceeding past the Spring Meeting House (Quaker), and then towards Lindley's Mill at a ford on Cane Creek (Cain Creek). Ultimately the road is extended and intersects the main highway to Cross Creek (Fayetteville) and then on to Wilmington. This will be a major route for commerce and travelers for many decades.

In the late 1760's the Regulator movement impacts the general Piedmont area. Internet postings mention Thomas Lindley being a Regulator. This has not been confirmed (which is very difficult). The Regulators are a unique group of men. They were (typically) very loyal to the King, but clearly and vehemently disliked the local corruption that was transpiring in Orange County, and other areas in the Piedmont. Ultimately a battle occurs between militia men (militia is a term meaning local citizens – not regular British military, e.g. Army) or local North Carolina men, led by Gov. William Tryon, and the Regulators (without any specific battle leader). This battle occurs May 16, 1771, and a park in Alamance County (Alamance Battleground Park) preserves this historical event and location. The battle site is not far from Lindley's Mill. To be clear, this was local citizen (Regulator) against, local citizen (militia) each armed and following their leader (although the Regulators did not have a fighting leader). After the battle (Regulators loose), Regulators (who legally were found guilty of treason) were forgiven if they swear allegiance to the King, and turn in their firearms. It should be clearly noted, that on the militia side, under the leadership of Gov. Tryon, all the officers (except Edmund Fanning) will soon become Patriot leaders, founding fathers, and Governors of this state, both during and after the War for Independence. Generally speaking, Regulators were either neutral or remained loyal, and fought against the War for Independence. Note the word – <u>generally</u> (**not all**). With the Pyle family, they were Regulators and Tories. If the Lindley family were regulators, the idea of Toryism is not that surprising, or at least a division of sentiment between relatives and friends.

Unfortunately, Hugh Laughlin dies in 1765. His exact date of death is unknown, however, Court Minutes assist, with this entry (May Tern 1765), *"....granted Mary Laughlin on the estate of Hugh Laughlin....deceased..."*. Many internet postings document his death by using his will's date of February 24, 1765. Yet, it seems that the will was written near his death, and implies that maybe he became very ill. Never the less, the Mill partnership continues with Mary Laughlin and Thomas Lindley.

Only two (Lindley) land transaction occurred during this period via Orange County deed records. The first one was Thomas Lindley dated December 9, 1768 (3/246). The oddity about this record was mentioning of buying land - which was already part of his land. Was he buying back his partners interest? – *"Frederick Gregg and Richard Lyons of Cumberland County, merchants on the one part and Thomas Lindley for in consideration of £45...part of the tract granted to Thomas Lindley from Granville dated February 22..."* No year listed. Here are the metes and bounds (abbreviated by me – P=poles=16.5 feet) *"...begin south fork of Cane Creek, southwest corner tree of the original tract, N78P to south fork of Cane Creek down creek 114P to a branch then up the branch 120P then west to the beginning..."* The other transaction was William Lindley purchasing 100 acres of land from Edmund Fanning for £55. The metes and bounds did not have a creek, and the preamble of the deed did not list the location, other than Orange County. There was one reference on the metes and bounds where the land adjoined "Davis". (Deed book 2, page 593- October 2, 1769.)

One marriage that is of interest, was John Lindley and Sarah Pyle (March 16, 1768). Sarah was 6th child of Dr. John Pyle of Chatham County. Dr. Pyle (already discussed in this book) was well known as a Loyalist Doctor, and resided south of the Lindley's (about a mile).

1780-1800

During this twenty year time-frame, the family will go through some difficult times. Parents would pass away, as well as children dieing in the war. After the war is over, and North Carolina settles down as a State, land sales will begin to increase.

James Lindley was a loyalist participating in the Battle of Kettle Creek (SC). He was hanged "as an example" in 1779. Certainly this was grievously accepted back home. Could his hanging propel his brother John into joining the Loyalist cause? Further, William, who was also a Tory, was ambushed and killed by local patriots.

The battle at Lindley's Mill occurs September 14, 1781. John Lindley, son of Thomas is a Tory officer serving under David Fanning during the battle at Lindley's Mill September 14, 1781. John is married to Dr. Pyle's daughter, Sarah. Dr. Pyle's son, John Pyle Jr., was the famous leader of men that got cut up in the event called – Pyle's Defeat. It was well documented that Dr. Pyle's son was maimed, and would not be able to fight again. Tradition states, that John Lindley's brother, Jonathan, was fighting on the Patriot side, opposite his brother.

Thomas Lindley dies September 14, 1781. Here is his will: "Thomas Lindley Will (1780) *"Whereas I Thomas Lindley of the County of Orange in North Carolina, being far advance in years*, [he would be 74 years old] *yet of sound mind and memory....I give and bequeath unto my beloved Ruth Lindly the sum of one hundred pounds together with all my household furniture except one feather bed and furniture and the privilege of the new end of the house I now dwell in securely and sufficiently maintained in necessary provisions and ??? firewood cut and drawed to her door also keeping for one horse and two cows and it is my will that she shall have the above mentioned privileges during her natural life in widowhood. I give and bequeath unto my son William Lindly two hundred acres of ??? part of the tract I now live on to be laid off for him in the following manner, beginning at a red oak the north west corner of the whole tract, running thence thirty three chains three yards and two feet south to a stake thence east sixty chains to a stake then north thirty three chains three yards and two feet to a post oak then west to the first station to him the said William Lindly his heirs… I give and bequeath unto my daughter Katherine White the sum of twenty pounds to her and heirs forever. I also give and bequeath unto all my other children (to wit) Thomas Lindly, Ruth Hadley, William Lindly, John Lindly Eleanor Morris and Deborah Newlin to each and ever of them the sum of twenty pounds to them and their heirs forever. I give and bequeath unto Jonathan Lindly the remainder of the tract of land or plantation whereon now dwell to him…that he shall ??? his mother the above privileges which I have bequeathed to her I also give unto my son Jonathan Lindly my still and one feather bed and furniture… I give and bequeath unto my grandson Thomas Lindley son of William Lindly the sum of ten pounds to be paid to him when he arises to the age of twenty one years, to them their heirs and assigns forever and I also give and bequeath unto Friends of Spring Meeting two acres of land whereon the Meeting House land to them and their heirs forever and it is my will that all the provision or overflow of my personal estate (if any thereby) after the above mentioned…shall be divided amongst my children….this fifteenth day of the third month in the year of our Lord one thousand seven hundred and eighty."* This will was proven in August Court 1782.

Some of the confusion in the upcoming history will be – which Thomas Lindley. It was Thomas Lindley's grandson, (Son, William's son) Thomas who purchased the Mill, and not Thomas Jr. William writes a will very soon before his death, and would allude to an illness. In fact, he writes the Will on September 22, 1784 and dies September 29th. In his will he writes (in the preamble) "…*calling to mind the uncertainty of time do this twenty second day of the ninth month…*" August 26, 1792 (4/601) Thomas Lindley – Executor of William Lindley deceased sells 270 acres to Jonathan Lindley for £80.0.0. This was part of the NC State Land grant dated November 17, 1790 which encompassed 290 acres of land.

In 1788 a number of State land grants were purchase by Jonathan Lindley, who has been documented as being a well known Patriot (although I do not have any specific information about his service).

About 1795 (cannot locate an exact date of death), Mary Laughlin dies. This causes four land transactions during the settlement of the estate. These four deeds are dated August 30, 1796, and include the wording - "*Will of Hugh Laughlin date Feb 24, 1765*", which was administered by the following people:

1) James Woody
2) James Allen
3) James Mathews
4) Allen Edwards
5) Nathaniel Morrison

6) John Hackney

The following are the four deeds:

1. (5/790) Jehu Pyle buys 84 acres on the south side of the mill land for £232.0.0 – Jehu is the youngest son of Dr. John Pyle in Chatham Co. **NOTE:** Jehu sells this exact tract of land to Allen Edwards in September (the day was left out of the deed record) 1796 for the same amount.

2. (9/161) Thomas Lindley buys the mill partnership (half-interest) for £251.0.0 – Now the Lindley family owns the mill 100% (former partnership).

3. (6/318) Allen Edwards buys 117 acres of land near the mill for £313.0.0

4. (8/342) Thomas Braxton Jr. buys 117 acres of land on Cain Creek for £330.0.0

During the 1800's, the Lindley family will continue to prosper and expand, by purchasing land in both Orange and Chatham County. As stated earlier, this book was not written as a family genealogy story book. To end this topic, it should be noted that some of the Lindley's move to Indiana – Orange County, Indiana. Be careful when reviewing family history, by overlooking the "two Orange Counties".

Several web sites document the Lindley family as being primarily loyal to the crown. However, Revolutionary War pensions document several Lindley's (outside of North Carolina) that fought for Independence. They are listed below:

- Caleb Lindley – Washington Co. PA – Private, Capt. Horton,
- Col Lindley NJ Militia
- Moses Lindley – NY, Private, Col Dayton 3rd NJ Regiment
- There are two MA pensions, but they were for a Lindsly/Lindsley (David and Hannah)

Land Deed Records

This section will detail the land holdings of the Lindley's, while in Orange County. Alamance County was formed from Orange in 1849.

For those who are not aware about the details of a "Granville Grant" here is part of the text. As you will discover, this is not just a grant of land you buy and move on. There are a lot of "strings attached" including yearly "rent".

".... Xxx acres of land: All which premises are more particularly described and set forth in the plan or map thereof hereunto annexed; together with all woods, underwoods, timber, and timber-trees, lakes, ponds, fishings, waters, water-courses, profits, commodities, appurtenances, and hereditaments whatsoever thereunto belonging, or in any-wise appertaining; together with the privilege of hunting, hawking, and fowling, and of taking, catching and making use of all sorts of game in and upon the premises hereby granted, and all mines and minerals whatsoever therein to be found, (except, and always reserved cut of this present grant unto the King's most excellent Majesty, his heirs and successors, one fourth part of all the Gold and Sliver mines to be found in or upon the said premise, and one Moiety or half part of all other mines and minerals whatsoever, and all white pine trees now growing, or hereafter to be found growing thereon) TO HAVE AND TO HOLD the said piece or parcel of land, and all and singular other the premises hereby granted, with the appurtenances, (except before excepted) unto the said _____ Heirs and Assigns, for ever; YIELDING AND PAYING therefore Yearly, and ever Year, for ever, unto the said Earl, his heirs and assigns, the yearly rent of sum of_____ which is at the rate of Three Shillings Sterling, or Four Shillings Proclamation money, for every hundred acres, at or upon the two most useful seats or days of payment in the year, that is to say the seat of the annunciation of the blesses Virgin Mary, and the seat of St. Michael the Archangel, in every year, by even and equal portions, and to be paid at the court-house of the County of _____ aforesaid, unto the said Early, or his deputy-attorney, or receiver, for the time being; the first payment thereof to be made on such of the said Seat-days, as shall first happen after the date hereof. And the said _____ for him, heirs, and assigns, and for every of them doth hereby covenant, promise, and agree, to and with the said Earl, his heirs and assigns, and to and with every of them, but those presents, in manner and form following: that is to say; that he the said _____ his heirs and assigns, shall and will Yearly, and every year, for ever, well and truly pay or cause to be paid unto the said Earl, his heirs and assigns, or unto his or their deputy-attorney, or receiver, for the time being, on the days, and at the place aforesaid, the aforesaid yearly rent or sum of _____ by half yearly payments, as aforesaid; and further, that he the said _____....within three years, to be accounted from the day of the date hereof, clear and cultivated, at the rate of three acres for every hundred acres of the said preemies hereby granted. PROVIDED always....that it shall happen that the said yearly rent of _____ or any part thereof..."

James Lindley Granville Grant #82 (1760)

There are two Granville land grants to James Lindley. Here is the 330 acre grant on Cane Creek. This land grant mentions (via the survey) Lambert and Harlet being on one corner of this land. The survey plat does not show a creek running on or through this parcel.

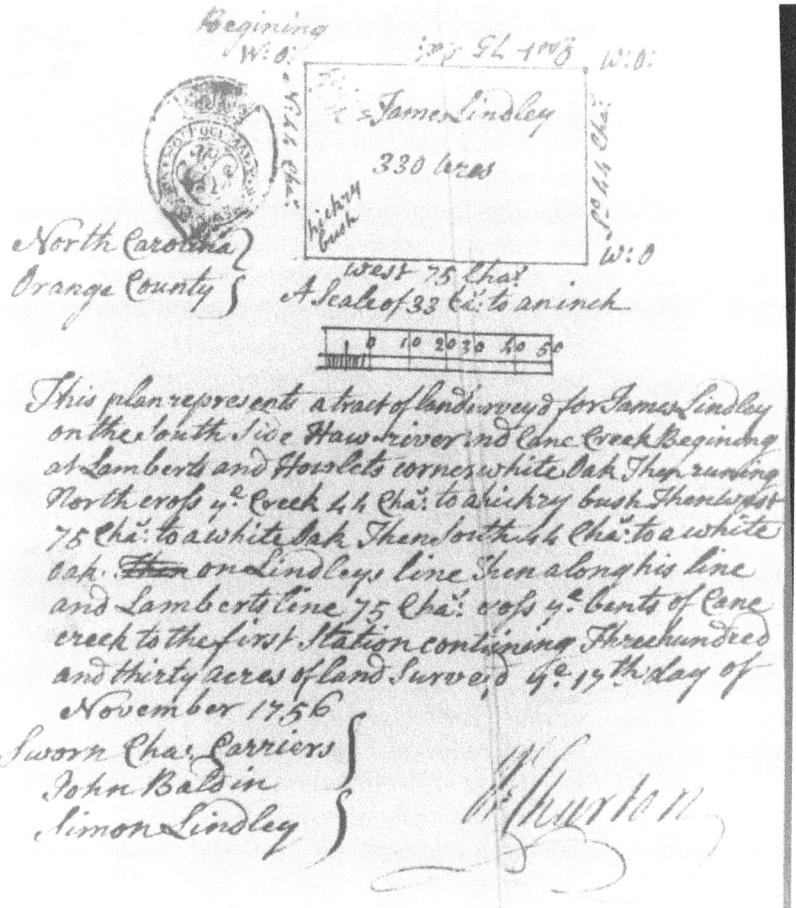
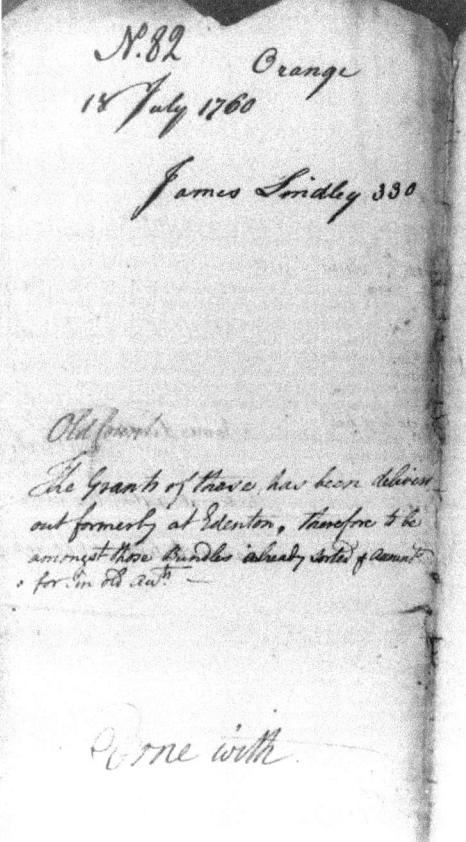

The grant, dates July 8, 1760.

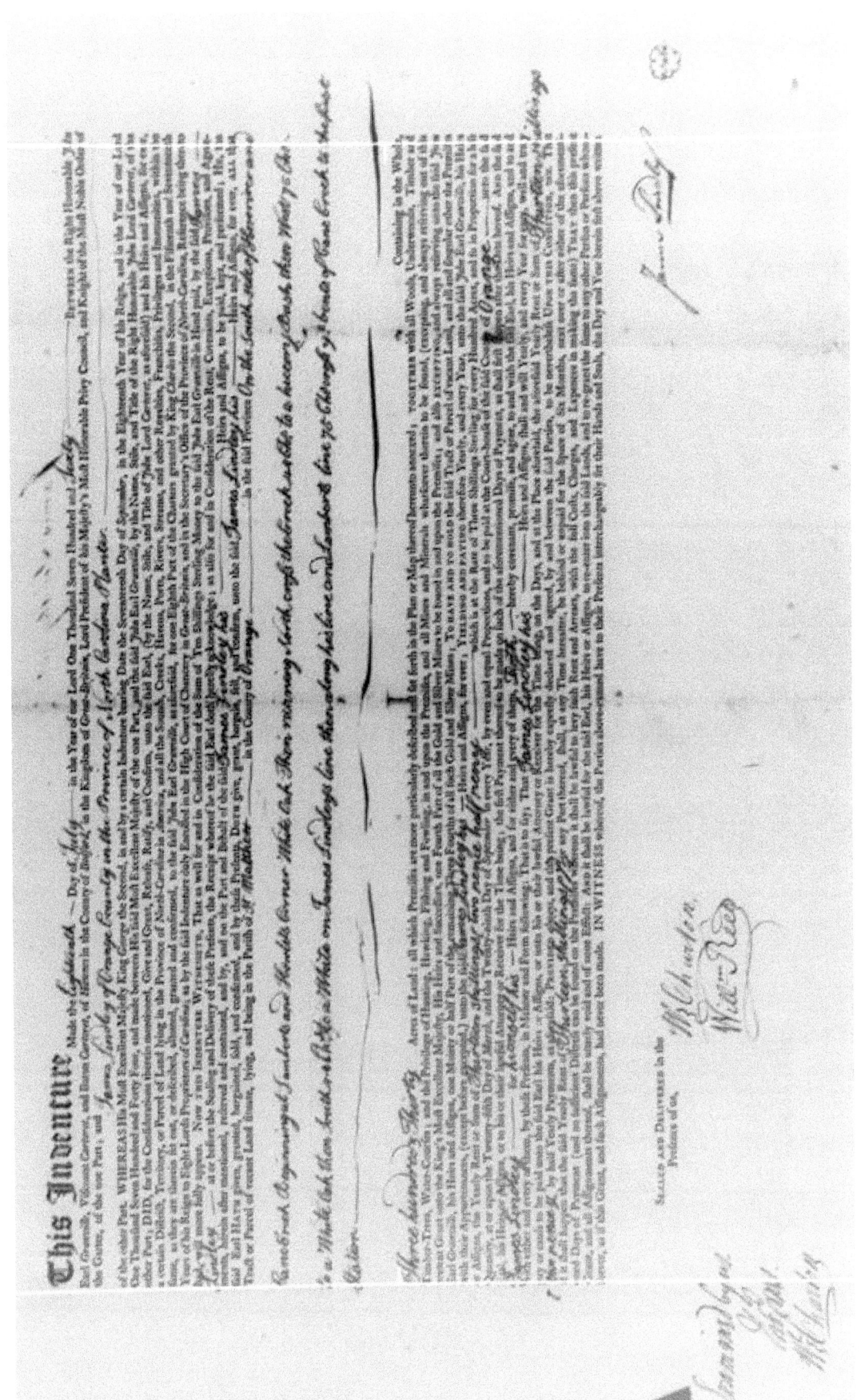

James Lindley Granville Grant #153 (1760)

Here is a grant for 200 acres on "Lick Branch", waters of Terrell's Creek.

This plan represents a tract of land Surveyd for James Lindley on lick branch ye waters of Terrels Creek & Begining at a black Oak bush Then running North 40 Cha: to a white Oak. Then west 50 Cha: to a white Oak Then South 40 Cha: to a Stake Then East 50 Cha: to the first Station containing Two hundred Acres of land Surveyd ye 16th day of November 1756 &

Sworn Cha: Carriers
Wm Braxon
John Baldin

Wm Churton

Ja: Lindley

No. 153 August 2. 1760

Counterpart

James Lindley 200

Orange

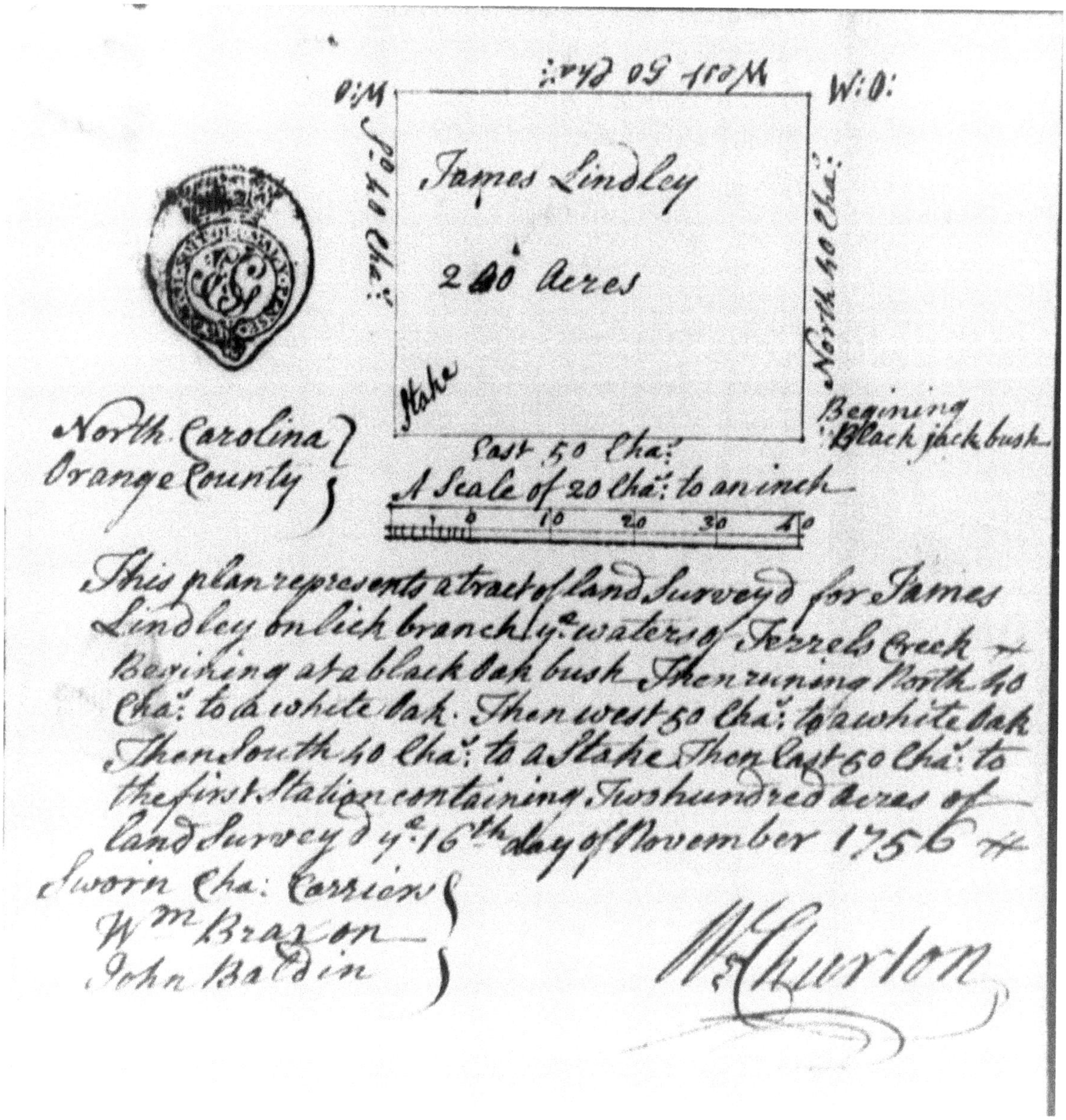

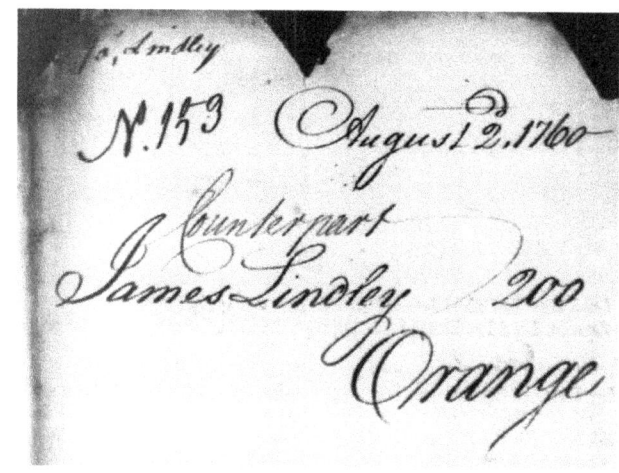

The grant dates August 2, 1760.

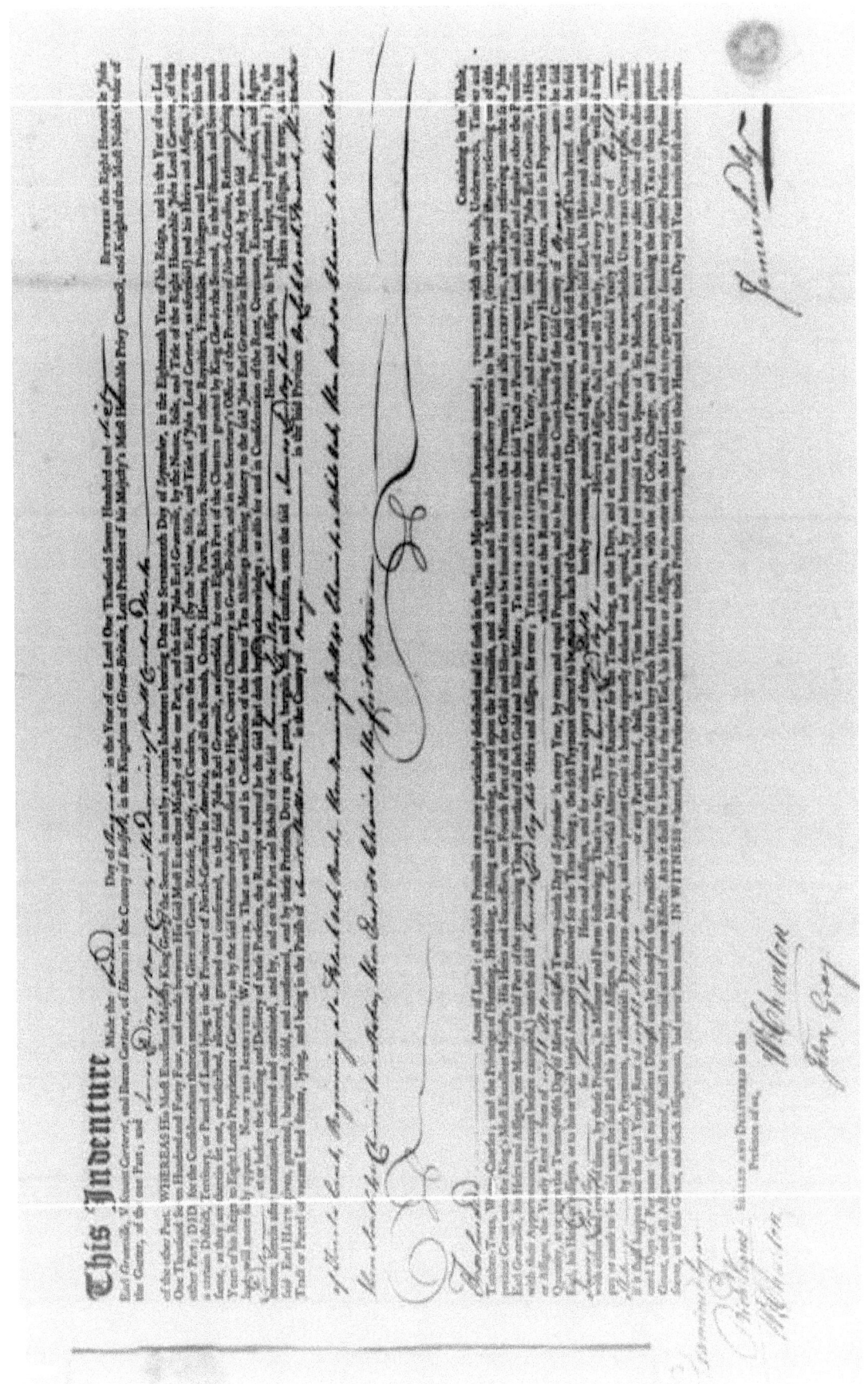

James Lindley Granville Grant (1760)

Here is a grant for 640 acres of land on both sides of Terrell's Creek and the mouth of Lick Branch.

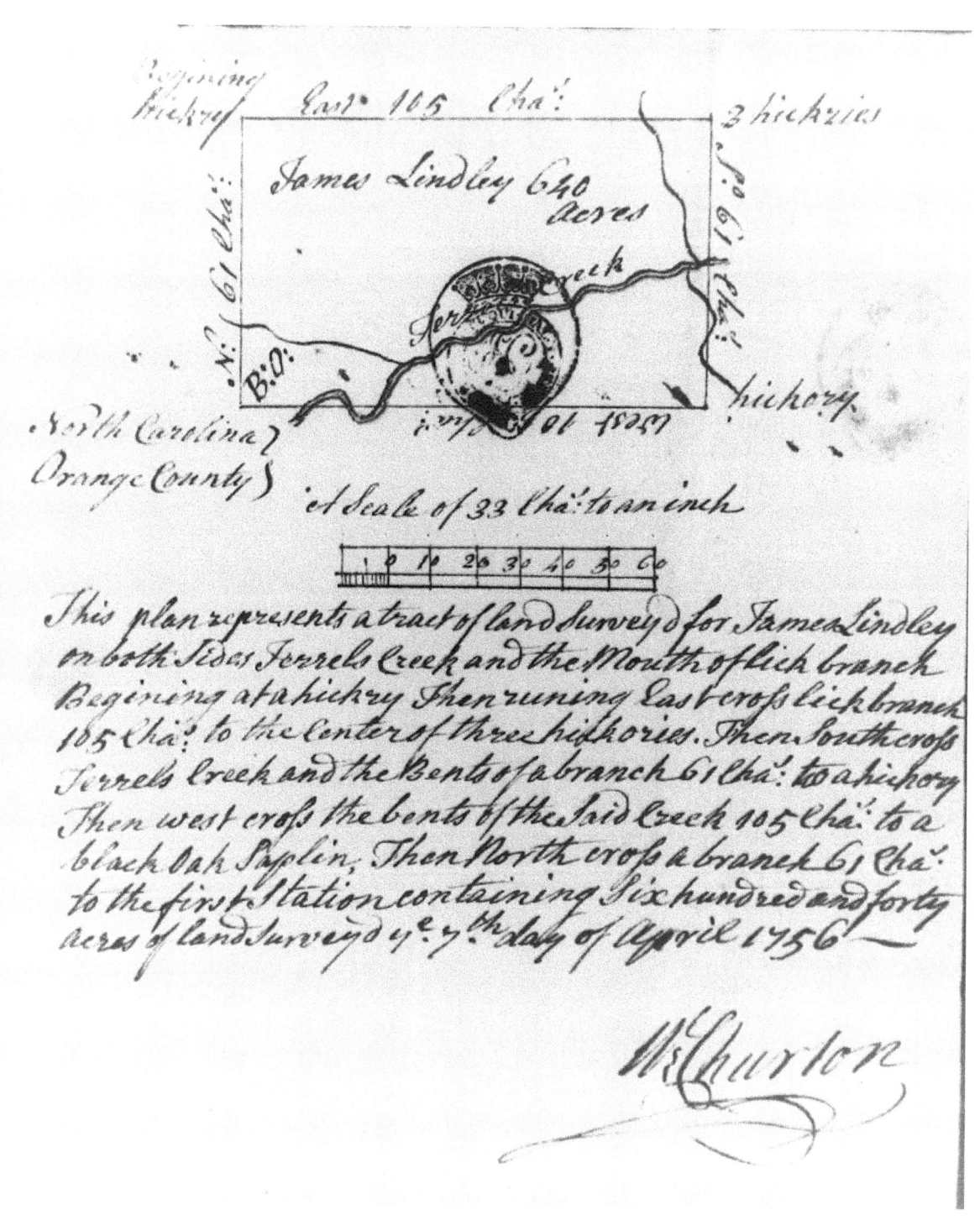

Grant dated January 8, 1761.

Here is a USGS map that might be the location of the Granville Grant. It is extremely difficult to use the grant's drawing to accurately locate the grant.

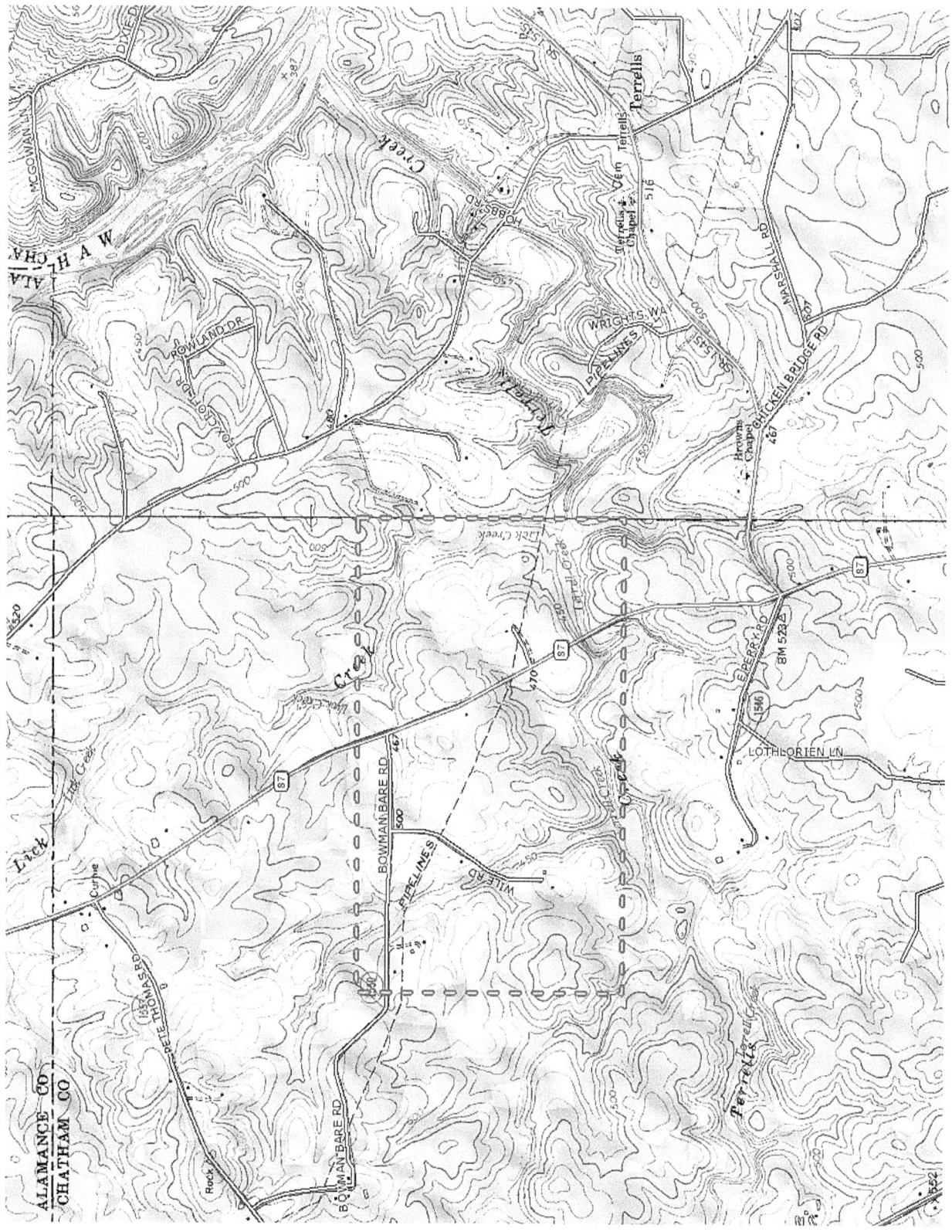

Thomas Lindley Granville Grant #66 (1759)

This 600 acre grant is on both sides of the South Fork of Cane Creek and on the west side of the Haw River. Surveyed May 8, 1756. There are two separate grant entries for this same 600 acres. Not sure why, as they are identical in wording and plat drawing, only one is included. (Below shows both entry numbers)

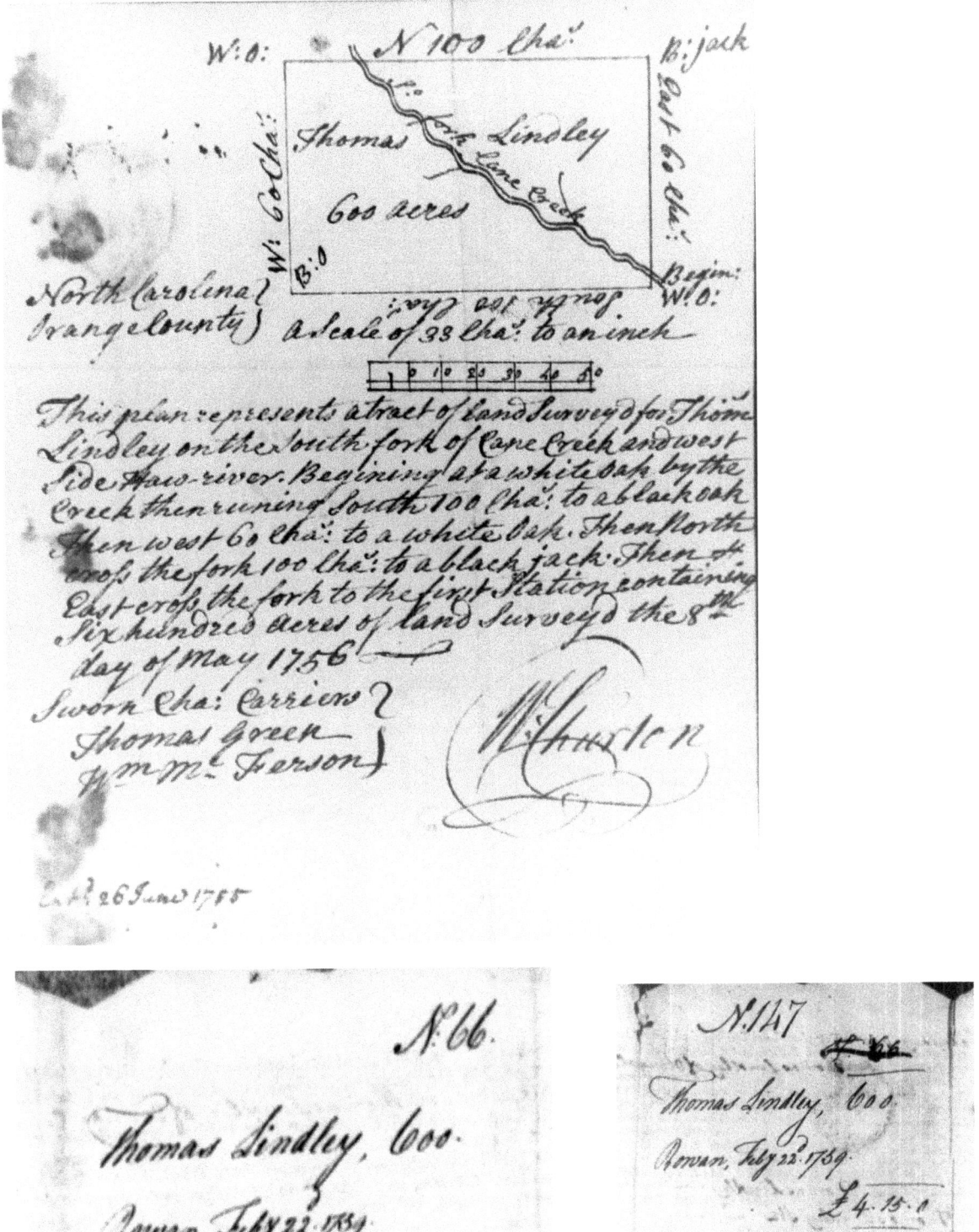

Close up.

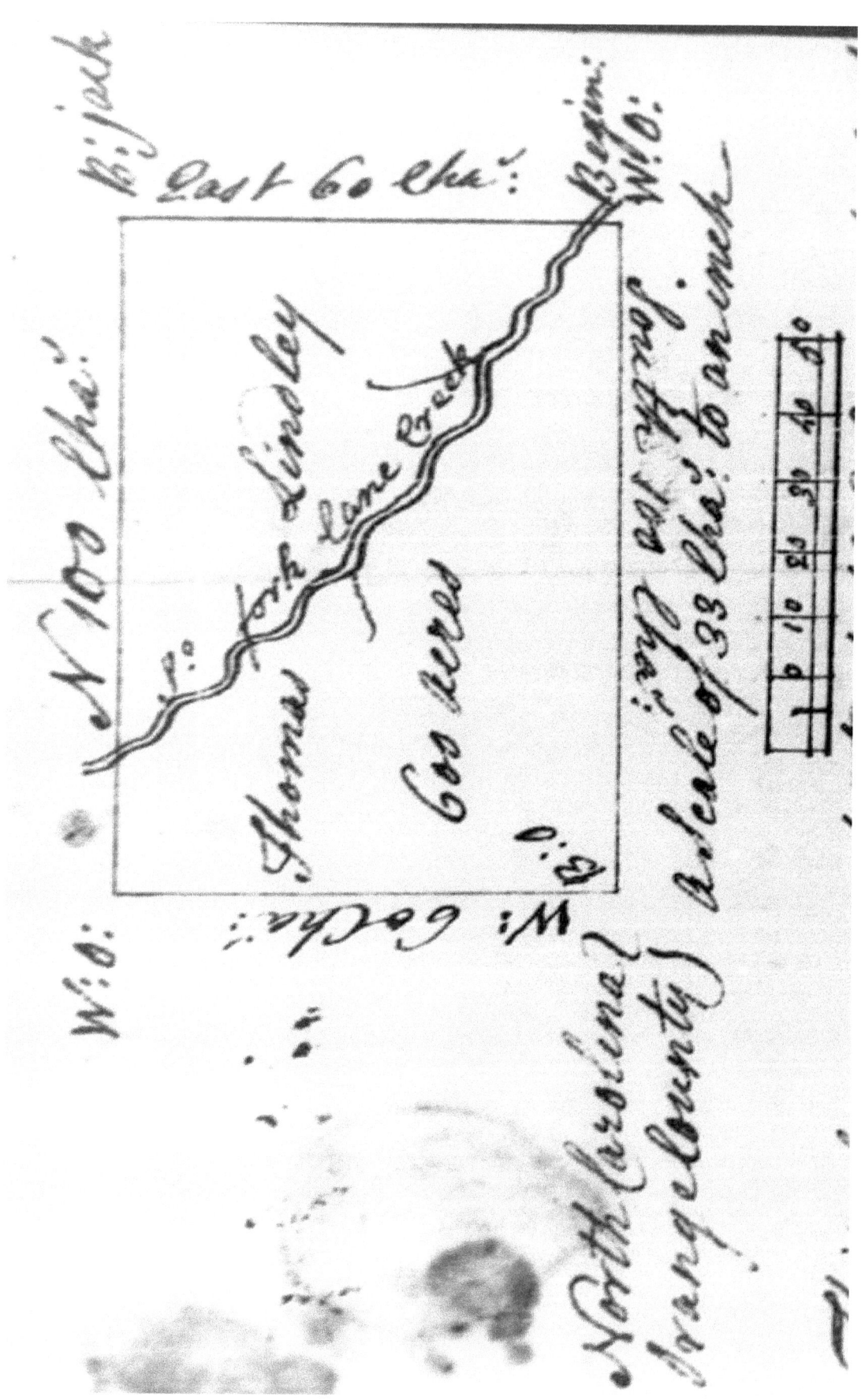

This modern map shows the location of the South Fork of Cane Creek, in an attempt to locate the Grant.

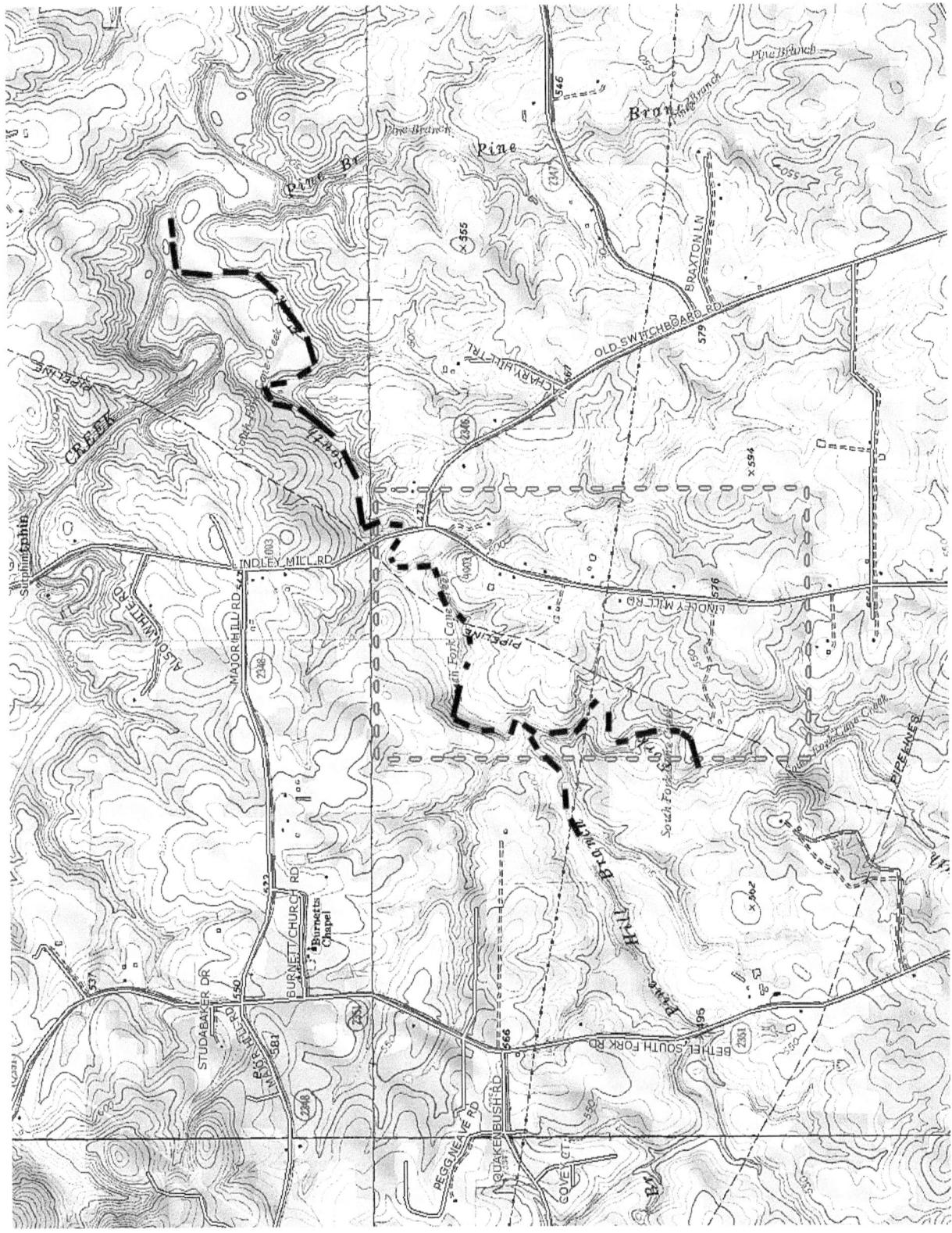

Grant dated February 22, 1759.

This Indenture, Made the Twenty Second Day of February in the Year of our Lord One Thousand Seven Hundred and Fifty Nine BETWEEN the Right Honourable John Earl Granville, Viscount Carteret, and Baron Carteret, of Hawnes, in the County of Bedford, in the Kingdom of Great-Britain, Lord President of His Majesty's Most Honourable Privy Council, and Knight of the Most Noble Order of the Garter, of the One Part, and Thomas Lindley of Orange County in Province of North of the other Part. WHEREAS His Most Excellent Majesty King GEORGE the Second, in and by a certain Indenture, bearing Date the Seventeenth Day of September, in the Eighteenth Year of his Reign, and in the Year of our Lord One Thousand Seven Hundred and Forty Four, and made between his said Most Excellent Majesty, of the One Part, and the said John Earl Granville, by the Name, Stile, and Title of the Right Honourable John Lord Carteret, of the other Part, DID, for the Considerations therein mentioned, Give and Grant, Release, Ratify, and Confirm, unto the said Earl, (by the Name, Stile, and Title of John Lord Carteret, as aforesaid,) and his Heirs and Assigns for ever, a certain District, Territory, or Parcel of Land, in North-Carolina, in America; and all the Squares, Creeks, Havens, Ports, Rivers, Streams, and other Royalties, Franchises, Privileges, and Immunities, within the same, as they are therein set out or described, allotted, and granted, and confirmed, to the said John Earl Granville, as aforesaid, for One Eighth Part of the Charters granted by King CHARLES the Second, in the Fifteenth and Seventeenth Years of his Reign, to Eight Lords Proprietors of Carolina, as by the said Indenture, duly Inrolled in the High Court of Chancery in Great-Britain, and in the Secretary's Office in North Carolina, Reference being thereto had, will more fully appear. NOW THIS INDENTURE WITNESSETH, That as well for and in Consideration of the Sum of Ten Shillings Sterling Money, to the said John Earl Granville, in Hand paid, by the said Thomas Lindley Heirs and Assigns, to be paid, kept, at or before the Sealing and Delivery of these Presents, the Receipt whereof is hereby acknowledged, as also for and in Consideration of the Rents, Covenants, Exceptions, Provisos, and Agreements herein after mentioned, reserved, and contained, and by and on the Part and Behalf of the said Thomas Lindley his Heirs and Assigns, to be paid, kept, and performed, he the said Earl HATH Given, Granted, Bargained, Sold, and Confirmed, and by these Presents, DOTH, from himself, and his Heirs, Give, Grant, Bargain, Sell and Confirm, unto the said Thomas Lindley his Heirs and Assigns for ever, all that Tract or Parcel of Land, situate, lying, and being in the Parish of St Matthew in the County of Orange in the said Province. On the North Fork of Cane Creek a West Side Haw River

Beginning at a white Oak by the Creek then running South 100 Chains to a Black Oak then West 50 Chains to a white Oak then North Gof the Fork 100 Chains to a Black Jack then East of the Fork to the first Station

Containing in the Whole Six Hundred Acres: All which said Premises are most particularly described and set forth in the Plan or Map thereof, hereunto annexed, together with all Woods, Underwoods, Timber, and Timber-Trees, Water-Courses, and the Privilege of Hunting, Hawking, Fishing, and Fowling, in and upon the Premisses, and all Mines and Minerals whatsoever, therein to be found, excepting and reserving always, out of this present Grant, and to the King's Most Excellent Majesty, his Heirs and Successors, One Fourth Part of all the Gold and Silver Mines, therein to be found; and also, excepting and always reserving thereout, unto the said John Earl Granville, one Moiety or Half Part of the remaining Three Fourths of all such Gold and Silver Mines; TO HAVE AND TO HOLD the said Tract or Parcel of Land; and all and singular other the Premisses, with their Appurtenances, (except as before excepted) unto the said Thomas Lindley his Heirs and Assigns for ever, YIELDING AND PAYING therefore, Yearly, and every Year, unto the said John Earl Granville, his Heirs and Assigns, the Yearly Rent of Seventy Four Shillings lawful Money, and the Twenty-fifth Day of March, and the Twenty-ninth Day of September, in every Year, by even or equal Portions, and to be paid at the Court-House for the said County of Orange unto the said Earl, his Heirs or Assigns, or to his or their lawful Attorney or Deputy-Receiver for the Time being; the first Payment thereof to be made on such of the aforementioned Days of Payment as shall first happen after the Date hereof; and the said Thomas Lindley for himself, his Heirs and Assigns, and for either and every of them DOTH hereby Covenant, Promise, and Agree, to and with the said Earl, his Heirs and Assigns, and to and with either or every of them, by these Presents, in Manner and Form following; That is to say, That the said Thomas Lindley his Heirs or Assigns, shall and will, Yearly, and every Year, for ever, well and truly pay, or cause to be paid unto the said Earl, his Heirs or Assigns, or unto his or their lawful Attorney or Deputy-Receivers for the Time being, on the Days, and at the Place aforesaid, the said Yearly Rent or Sum of Seventy Four Shillings by half Yearly Payments, as aforesaid: Provided always, and this present Grant is hereby expressly Declared and Agreed, by and between the said Parties, to be, nevertheless, UPON THIS CONDITION, viz. That if it shall happen, that the said Yearly Rent of Seventy four Shillings or any Part thereof, shall at any Time hereafter, be behind or unpaid for the Space of Six Months next over or after any of the aforementioned Days of Payment, (and no sufficient Distress can be found on the Premisses, to levy such Rent and Arrears, with the full Costs, Charges and Expences in making the same) That then, this present Grant, and all Affignments thereof, shall be utterly void, and of none Effect; and it shall be lawful for the said Earl, his Heirs or Assigns, to re-enter into the said Lands, and to re-possess the same, to any other Person or Persons whomsoever, as if this Grant, and such Assignments thereof, had never been made. IN WITNESS whereof, the Parties above-named, have hereunto set their Hands and Seals, the Day and Year first above written.

Thomas Lindley

Signed, Sealed and Delivered
in the Presence of Us,

W Churton
Thomas Jones

Hugh Laughlin Granville Grant #60 (1753)

Hugh Laughlin receives this grant for 640 acres before the Lindley's. This one square mile of land resides on "Cain Creek".

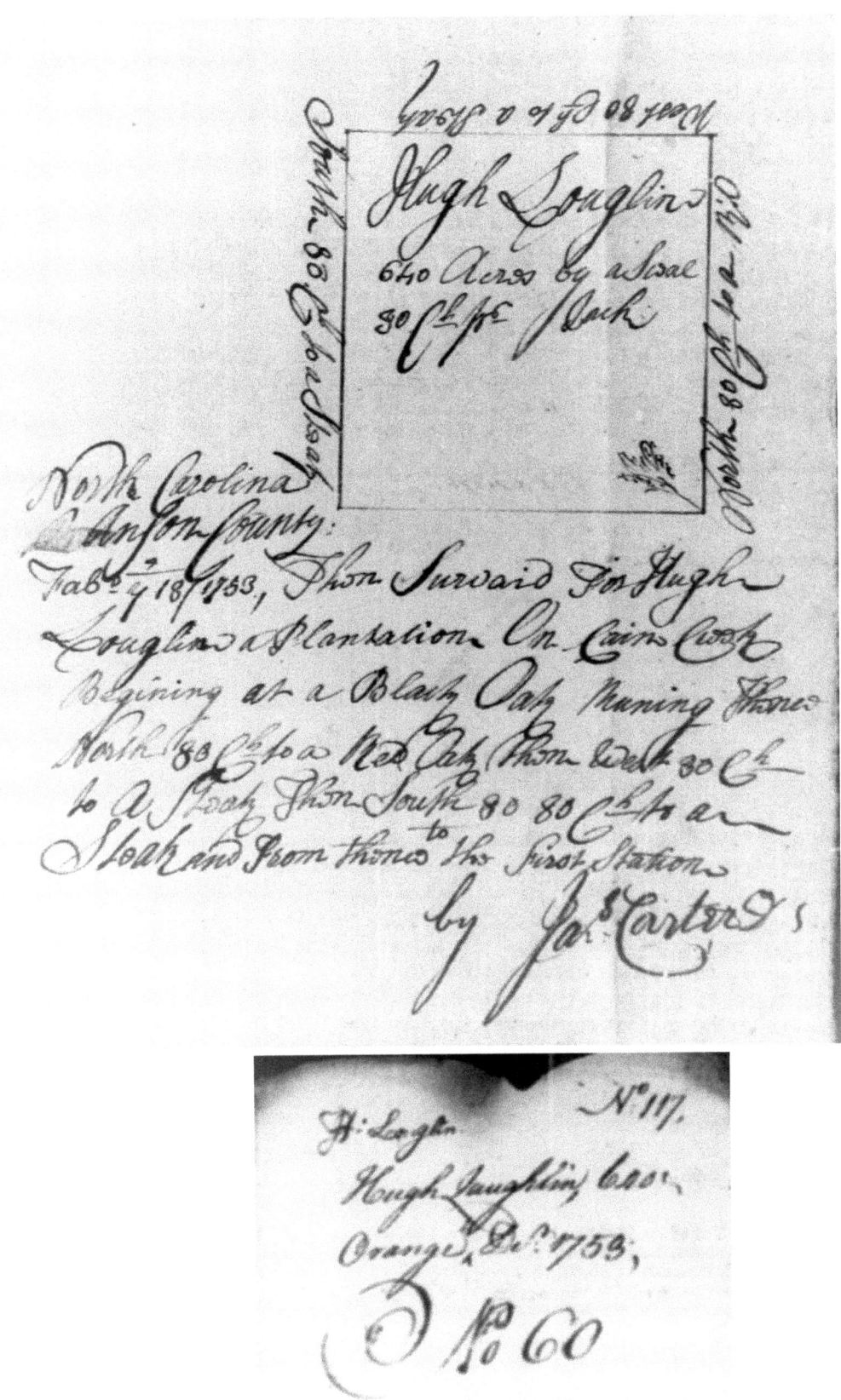

Grant dated, December 4, 1753.

Mill Specific (History)

It all begins with the very first record, well documenting the partnership and creation of the mill. Book 1, page 35, Orange County. *"...between Hugh Laughlin and Thomas Lindley to become copartners and in joint company to erect and build a water grist mill on Cane Creek on the south side of the Haw River in said County and on a piece and parcel of land belonging to said Hugh Laughlin and the said Thomas Lindley situated on the line of the partners so that the water is to be take out of that part of land belonging to the said Hugh Laughlin and the sat for the mill to be on that part of the land belonging to the said Thomas Lindly containing in the whole 3 acres...beginning at a persimmon tree on the north side of Cane Creek then east 30P to a post oak then south the shell bark hickory on south side of said creek 20P then west to a sweet gum 30P then 30p to the first station....make a just and equal division of all and singular the species, interest and profits arising in and by the said mill and premises.."*

Hugh Laughlin dies (1765), but his wife continues as owner of the mill. Thomas Lindley dies in 1781, and the partnership ends. It isn't clear how the mill operation is transferred, except Jonathan and William are executors of the estate. However, when Laughlin's widow dies, a grandson of Thomas Lindley (son of William, who was the son of Thomas Lindley) bought half interest (for £251) in the mill from the Laughlin Estate (Deed book 9, page, 161). The mill remained in the Lindley family until 1844. William Lindley (son of Thomas – who purchased the ½ from the heirs of the Laughlin estate) sells the mill (September 17, 1844) and 60 acres of land to Paris Benbow (Orange County Deed book 31, page 431) for $2,300. Benbow purchases more of the surrounding land as well (see deed references following).

Alamance County is formed from the western side of Orange County in 1849. From now on, the mill will be located in Alamance County (all references to deed books will now be in Alamance County)

Paris Benbow sells the mill to John Dixon for $3,700 (Book 2 page 6) September 20, 1854. After almost 30 years, John Dixon (heirs) sell the mill to Joshua Perry for $2,000 (Book 10, page 274) December 15, 1883. This sale included 20 acres of land.

Joshua Perry dies intestate, and the estate liquidates the property to pay debt. The mill is auctioned off, and Robert L Sutphin purchases it for $1,275. In the deed (Book 12 page 35) it states the mill was known as the *Benbow Mill*. Then on July 29, 1889 Jonathan Thompson purchases a ½ interest in the mill for $1,200 (Book 13, page 490). Almost ten years later, Thompson buys the remaining interest for $1,600 (Book 16, page 232), becoming the full owner of the mill.

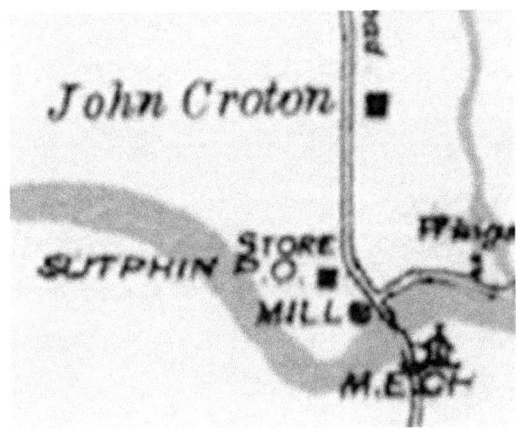

Throughout the early deeds, the Mill is referenced as a Saw Mill and Merchant Mill or Saw Mill and Grist Mill. It is interesting to note the "saw mill". During the transcription work in the N.C. State Archives (County Records) a folder was located that included old mill petitions. In this collection was an undated mill petition for Jonathan Lindley. He was requesting to erect a Merchant Mill on Cain Creek. Based on the paper and age, etc., it is estimated that this document dates to the late 1790's to early 1800's. It is possible that Jonathan expanded the mill complex to include a saw mill. However, a saw mill requires different power than a grist mill. Generally speaking, a grist mill operates at a relatively low R.P.M. whereas a saw mill demands a higher R.P.M. to operate the saw mechanics. Based on Millwright handbooks (from the 1800's) they recommend a "flutter wheel" to operate a saw mill. These are very wide wheels with a small diameter, thus the higher R.P.M. The point is, adding a saw mill operation was not simply adding a saw blade to the existing mechanics.

The only oddity was (why) the petition. Is it possible he was attempting to add a second dam?

For those interested, here are the metes and bounds of the mill property, from the 1850's: *"…beginning about 2 rods below the old ford and with the Hillsboro Road, N50ºE 12 poles to a turn in said road, then N86ºE 29 poles to a Spanish Oak on top of a ridge, then N10ºW 42 poles to a stone about 2 poles north east of the Miller Spring then S60ºW 75 poles to a birch on the north bank of the mill race then with the said old race to the pond, then with the pond and Willis Darks line and the creek to the beginning…"* (Note: a pole = 16.5 feet)

(Left s a diagram illustrating a flutter wheel)

Deed Records (Date Order) – 1755-1799

From	To		Date	Year	Book	Price	Acres	Description
Lindley	James	Downing	25-Jul	1755	1/49	£20.0.0	100	N-side of Cane Creek adj Downing - VA currency/granville grant
Laughlin	Hugh	Lindley	10-Aug	1755	1/35	NA	NA	** Mill agreement **
Lyon	Richard	Lindley	9-Dec	1768	3/246	£45.0.0	70	Fred Gregg&Rich Lyon Cumberland Co. s fork Cain Creek
Fanning	Edmond	Lindley	2-Oct	1769	2/593	£55.0.0	100	No location, but adjoins "Davis"
Lindley	John	Lewis	1-Feb	1781	12/33	NA	NA	Mary's Creek adj Widow Stanfield & Manors - no metes bounds
Lindley	Jonathan & Deborah	Stout	13-Jan	1786	4/283	£224.0.0	120.5	N. side Cane Creek - granville grant of John Jones 1754
North Carolina		Lindley	12-Jul	1788	4/117		130	#879 Land Grant on Cane Creek
Lindley	Jonathan	Morrison		1790	5/326	£0.5.0	5.5	Spring Meeting House prop, Thomas willed to son Jonathan
Woody	James	Lindley	21-Feb	1792	4/541	£130.0.0	167	Part of his Granville Grant (8/15/1759) on Marys Creek
Brooks	John	Lindley	14-Apr	1792	4/609	£300.0.0	300	Both sides Cane Creek, Granville grant (8/7/1760)
Lindley	William	Lindley	26-Aug	1792	4/601	£80.0.0	270	Dead William's estate, part of his grant (11/17/1790)
Dicks	Zachareih	Lindley		1792	4/525	£24.0.0	16	Part of his State Grant of 770a (7/10/1788)
Austin	Solomon ETAL	Lindley	8-Mar	1794	5/98	£250.0.0	265	Little Cain Creek (see 5/189)
Lindley	Mirriam & Thomas	Crutchfield	20-Mar	1794	8/203	£305.0.0	65.0	Little Cain Creek adjacent to Wortham
Lindley	Thomas Sr.	Lindley	11-Oct	1794	5/189	£30.0.0	265	Waters of Little Cain Creek, adj Fred Williams & Joe Weeks
Ray	John	Lindley	14-Apr	1796	5/678	£25.0.0	37	Cain Creek adjoining McPhearson and Laughlin
Stockard	James	Lindley	9-Jun	1796	5/683	£110.0.0	175	on Great Alamance from William Ray Sr. 3/4/1793
Ray	William	Lindley	9-Jun	1796	5/677	£200.0.0	150	Great Alamance, adj Stockard - land to R. Ray Jr
Holliday	Henry	Lindley	16-Jun	1796	9/96	£10.0.0	21	(Thomas son of William deceased) waters of Cain Creek
Laughlin Etal		Braxton	30-Aug	1796	8/342	£330.0.0	117	On Cain Creek (Laughlin Death)
Laughlin Etal		Edwards	30-Aug	1796	6/318	£313.0.0	117	North side of Cane Creek (Laughlin Death)
Laughlin Etal		Lindley	30-Aug	1796	9/161	£251.0.0		1/2 interst in Mill (due to Laughlin death)
Laughlin Etal		Pyle	30-Aug	1796	5/790	£232.0.0	84	South of the mill land along the line of the dam (Laughlin death)
Pyle	Jehu	Edwards	1-Sep	1796	5/674	£232.0.0	84	South of the mill land along the line of the dam
Lochart	William	Owen	29-Nov	1796	5/774	£87.10.0	36.7	Adjacent to John McCollams plated 2/18/1788
North Carolina		Owen	8-Dec	1796	9/374		200	#1422 adjacent to Owen and Ward
Hart	Stephen	Lindley	5-Jan	1797	6/315	£90.0.0	60.5	William Whiteheads line called Lot #3 and #4
Lindley	Owen	Whitted Jr.	10-Jun	1797	6/96	$251	60.0	Eno River adj to Finley (Stephen Hart former land)
Clark	William	Lindley	6-Aug	1797	7/98	£350.0.0	200	Adjacent Eno River east side of Haw River
Hunter	Matthew	Lindley	20-May	1798	10/94	$900	316	Granville grant fro his dad (9/22/1762) to son (2/29/1793) Haw
Hunter	Matthew	Lindley	20-May	1798	10/94	$900	316	On Haw River
Lindley	Jonathan	Harvey	13-Jul	1798	14/330	$500	70.0	Land and 1/2 ownership in the Mill
Byrnes	Mary	Lindley	15-Oct	1798	10/338	NA	NA	in the index, not in the book
North Carolina		Lindley	17-Jun	1799	12/50		370	#1509 on Mary's Creek

Deed Records (Date Order) – 1800-1809

From	To	Date	Year	Book	Price	Acres	Description
Marshall	Jacob	Lindley	Jonathan	11-Jan	1800	8/311	$50	200	Varnell's Creek
Lindley	Grace & Owen	Findley	Hugh	3-Aug	1800	11/176	$40	5.5	Eno part of the tract Owen lives on
Findley	Hugh	Lindley	Owen	30-Aug	1800	10/21	$160	25.5	adjancent to Owen and Finley's part of tract Owen lives on
Horner	George	Lindley	Jonathan	18-Apr	1801	10/14	$1,200	425	McGowan's Creek
Patton	William	Lindley	Jonathan	8-Jul	1801	10/56	$150	70	150 milled spanish dollars - Varnell's Creek
Patton	John	Lindley	Jonathan	29-Sep	1802	10/258	$40	10	Adj to Jonathan Lindley and Ray's Spring Branch
Sharp	Aaron	Lindley	Jonathan	9-Oct	1802	10/337	$425	250	Rock Creek
Green	Edmond	Lindley	Jonathan	14-Jan	1803	10/336	$425	160	Varnell's Creek
Holliday	Henry	Lindley	Thomas	4-Feb	1803	10/344	£475.0.0	311	On Cain Creek
Morrow	James	Lindley	William	22-Apr	1803	10/376	£162.10.0	200	May Creek (not sure if this was to be Mary's Creek)
Lindley	Jonathan	Marris	John	23-May	1803	10/352	$425	160.0	Varnell's Creek
North Carolina		Lindley	Jonathan	4-Jan	1804	11/105		150	#1696 on May Creek
North Carolina		Lindley	William	4-Jan	1804	11/104		200	#1695 on Money's Creek
Clendenin	Joseph	Lindley	Jonathan	20-Feb	1804	11/142	£285.0.0	200	Varnell's Creek
Lindley	Jonathan	Holliday	Samuel	24-Feb	1804	11/143	$500	5.0	Land and 1/2 ownership in the Mill
Faucett	Henry	Lindley	Owen	16-May	1804	12/54	$90	23	1/7 part of James Findley east Eno River
Faucett	William	Lindley	Owen	26-May	1804	12/23	$90	23	another 1/7 part of James Findley east Eno River
Ray	Robert	Lindley	Jonathan	1-Aug	1804	13/222	$168	56	Tract from John Patton (8/29/1802) adj Lindley land
Watters	Jacob	Lindley	Jonathan	14-Nov	1804	12/55	$200	152	Jacob was from Granville co, Jonathan - Chatham, on Eno River
Christmas	Charles	Lindley	Jonathan	11-Mar	1805	12/298	$1,000		On Cane Creek, deceased John Christmas, off Moccasin Creek
North Carolina		Lindley	Jonathan	28-Nov	1805	12/50		48	#1731 NW of Jonathan's land
Morrow	James	Lindley	Jonathan	22-Feb	1806	12/255	$1,300	508	2-tracts, South Haw-266a, other land 242acres
Morrow	Andrew	Lindley	Jonathan	8-Mar	1806	12/254	$650	29	On Cain Creek
Thompson	James	Lindley	Jonathan	8-Mar	1806	12/257	$800	230	Varnell's Creek
May	Ludwick	Lindley	Jonathan	29-Jul	1806	12/256	$20	NA	Varnell's Creek - estate of John Campbell - deceased
Cate	James	Lindley	Jonathan	6-Sep	1806	12/292	$1,200	190	Marshall Creek
Patton	James	Lindley	Jonathan	22-Oct	1806	12/258	$200	370	Varnell's Creek (320a) and Dry Branch (50a)
Williams	James	Lindley	Jonathan	27-Oct	1806	12/259	NA	468	Haw River - south side
Berry	Elizabeth	Lindley	Jonathan	28-Oct	1806	12/260	$20	30	land of deceased Isaac Berry on great falls called Ellis Falls
Lindley	Jonathan	McPhearson	Enoch	21-Feb	1807	13/52	$150	37.0	adjacent to Widow Laughlin on Cane Creek
Carter Jr.	John	Lindley	William	25-Feb	1807	12/308	$600	150	land near road to John Thompson's Mill
Lindley	William	Johnston	William	27-Nov	1807	13/120	$1,800	600	Waters of the Haw
Campbell	Richard	Lindley	William	29-Dec	1807	13/264	$600	150	payment schedule listed in this deed to 1811
Whitsman	Conrod	Lindley	Jonathan	24-Jun	1809	13/222	£48.7.0	51	land on Bone Creek
Thompson	John	Lindley	Jonathan	15-Nov	1809	13/282	$100	150	on Whiteheads Creek

Deed Records (Date Order) – 1810-1850

From		To		Date	Year	Book	Price	Acres	Description
Lindley	Jonathan	Hunter	Robert	8-Jan	1810	13/405	$1,500	360.0	Land bought from Mat Hunter
Lindley	Jonathan	McPhearson	James	22-Feb	1810	13/508	$600	100.0	Cain Creek
Lindley	Jonathan	McPhearson	John	14-Apr	1810	13/508	$1,500	234.0	Cain Creek and mouth of Browns Spring branch
Lindley	Jonathan	Newlin	Nathenial	20-Apr	1810	13/417	$700	86.0	Bank of Haw River
Lindley	Jonathan	Woody	John	20-Apr	1810	13/418	$500	86.0	Bank of Haw River
Thompson	James	Lindley	Owen	23-Apr	1810	13/350	£150.0.0	142	Eno River - James Thompson deceased land
Lindley	Owen	Thompson	James	23-Apr	1810	13/409	£3.10.0	120.0	West Eno River
Lindley	Jonathan	Davis	Thomas	1-May	1810	13/383	$2,000	16.0	Cane Creek part of Zachariah Dicks
Lindley	Jonathan	Stanford	Richard	17-May	1810	13/361	$1,500	190.0	On Cane Creek
Lindley	Jonathan	Howard	Thomas	21-May	1810	13/539	$1,400	300.0	On Cane Creek
Lindley	Owen	Lindley	James	1-Jun	1810	13/419	$1,600	403.0	Eno River plantation Owen now lives on
Lindley	Jonathan	Lindley	John	2-Jun	1810	13/417	$800	348.0	McGowan's Creek
Lindley	Thomas	Bean	Thomas	5-Jun	1810	13/397	$1,000	200.0	Eno River willed to William Clark bu his deceased father
Lindley	John	Wood	Levi	4-Sep	1810	13/509	$1,250	250.0	On Rock Creek
Lindley	Jonathan	Murphy	Archibald	7-Sep	1810	13/492	$1,464	393.0	West Haw River south side of Alamance
Lindley	Jonath	Foust	Mary	27-Dec	1810	14/127	$600	129.0	adjacent to Mary Foust
Lindley	Jonathan	McPhearson	James	24-Mar	1811	13/480	$50	7.0	Cant read the creek name
Lindley	Jonathan	Foust	Daniel	24-Apr	1811	13/539	$850	220.0	adjacent to Mary Foust & Jacob Marshall
Lindley	Jonathan	Newlin	John	27-Apr	1811	13/540	$1,300	550.0	On Mary's Creek
Lindley	Thomas	Alston	Joseph	1-May	1811	17/112	$5,000	617	On Cane Creek adjacent to mill property
Lindley	Jonathan	Pennington	Levi	1-May	1811	13/538	$800	230.0	Clendinin Creek where Sam Chambers lived
Lindley	William	Campbell	Richard	18-May	1812	14/136	$600	150	Near the road to Thompson's Mill (William is in IN)
Lindley	Jonathan	Lawrence	James	2-Jun	1812	14/563	$600	96.0	South side of Cane Creek land from John Brooks
Lindley	Jonathan	Braxton	William	2-Jul	1812	14/150	$300	298.0	Braxton of Chatham Co, William Lindley deceased
Lindley	Jonathan	Wilson	Edward	17-Oct	1812	26/70	$600	234.0	(Jonathan of Chatham Co.) Eno River
Lindley	James	Faucett	James	Feb-29	1812	15/61	$40	18	Eno River
Lindley	John	McCracken	John	17-Jun	1814	14/741	$460	230.0	McGowan's Creek
Lindley	James	Faucett	James	27-Sep	1815	16/29	$1,080	360	Both side of Eno River
Lindley	Jonathan	Warren	William	20-Aug	1817	16/74	$50	50.0	Dry Branch
Lindley	Jonathan	Bobbitt	William	18-Aug	1820	18/279	$550	242.0	On Mary's Creek
Lindley	Jonathan	McDaniel	John	28-Feb	1822	18/200	$75	320.0	law suit collect debt of Luke Peacock - Verrial Creek
Lindley	Jonathan	Newlin	John	22-Apr	1822	19/366	NA	NA	Jonathan Lindley of Indiana appointing Newlin to collect debt
Lindley	Jonathan	Foust	John	22-May	1822	20/50	$250	220.0	(Jonathan of IN) Marys Creek
Lindley	Margaret & Thomas	Buckingham	Joseph	25-Nov	1822	21/159	Love	NA	Margaret is widow of Joe Buckinham Sr. give to her son 1/2
McPhearson	Stephen	Lindley	Joshua	22-Jan	1831	25/135	312	104	Estate of McPhearson Sarah Dixon involved Cane to Chatham line
Lindley	William	Richardson	Richie	15-Nov	1842	30/293	$550	232	On Cane Creek
Lindley	William	Zachory	Jonathan	27-Nov	1842	30/289	$650	182	on Cane Creek
Lindley	William	Benbow	Paris	17-Sep	1844	31/431	$2,300	60	Sells the Grist Mill and Land
Braxton	Hiram	Lindley	Jonathan	21-Aug	1845	34/458	$5	1.5	west side of Alamance Road, N side of Mill pond by pond
Lindley	Joshua	Clark	Alexander	1-Nov	1847	32/541	$512	104.0	(Josha of Chatham Co) Cane Creek
Lindley	Ella & A.H.	Benbow	Paris	25-Sep	1850	34/550	$1,250	62.0	Alamance Co. adj his other land and Braxton

Deed Records (Lindley Grantee)

From		To	Date	Year	Book	Price	Acres	Description
Lindley	Owen	James	1-Jun	1810	13/419	$1,600	403.0	Eno River plantation Owen now lives on
Lindley	Jonathan	John	2-Jun	1810	13/417	$800	348.0	McGowan's Creek
North Carolina		Jonathan	12-Jul	1788	4/117		130	#879 Land Grant on Cane Creek
Woody	James	Jonathan	21-Feb	1792	4/541	£130.0.0	167	Part of his Granville Grant (8/15/1759) on Marys Creek
Brooks	John	Jonathan	14-Apr	1792	4/609	£300.0.0	300	Both sides Cane Creek, Granville grant (8/7/1760)
Lindley	William	Jonathan	26-Aug	1792	4/601	£80.0.0	270	Dead William's estate, part of his grant (11/17/1790)
Dicks	Zachareih	Jonathan		1792	4/525	£24.0.0	16	Part of his State Grant of 770a (7/10/1788)
Ray	John	Jonathan	14-Apr	1796	5/678	£25.0.0	37	Cain Creek adjoining McPhearson and Laughlin
Stockard	James	Jonathan	9-Jun	1796	5/683	£110.0.0	175	on Great Alamance from William Ray Sr. 3/4/1793
Ray	William	Jonathan	9-Jun	1796	5/677	£200.0.0	150	Great Alamance, adj Stockard - land to R. Ray Jr
Hunter	Matthew	Jonathan	20-May	1798	10/94	$900	316	Granville grant fro his dad (9/22/1762) to son (2/29/1793) Haw
Hunter	Matthew	Jonathan	20-May	1798	10/94	$900	316	On Haw River
Byrnes	Mary	Jonathan	15-Oct	1798	10/338	NA	NA	in the index, not in the book
North Carolina		Jonathan	17-Jun	1799	12/50		370	#1509 on Mary's Creek
Marshall	Jacob	Jonathan	11-Jan	1800	8/311	$50	200	Varnell's Creek
Horner	George	Jonathan	18-Apr	1801	10/14	$1,200	425	McGowan's Creek
Patton	William	Jonathan	8-Jul	1801	10/56	$150	70	150 milled spanish dollars - Varnell's Creek
Patton	John	Jonathan	29-Sep	1802	10/258	$40	10	Adj to Jonathan Lindley and Ray's Spring Branch
Sharp	Aaron	Jonathan	9-Oct	1802	10/337	$425	250	Rock Creek
Green	Edmond	Jonathan	14-Jan	1803	10/336	$425	160	Varnell's Creek
North Carolina		Jonathan	4-Jan	1804	11/105		150	#1696 on May Creek
Clendenin	Joseph	Jonathan	20-Feb	1804	11/142	£285.0.0	200	Varnell's Creek
Ray	Robert	Jonathan	1-Aug	1804	13/222	$168	56	Tract from John Patton (8/29/1802) adj Lindley land
Watters	Jacob	Jonathan	14-Nov	1804	12/55	$200	152	Jacob was from Granville co, Jonathan - Chatham, on Eno River
Christmas	Charles	Jonathan	11-Mar	1805	12/298	$1,000		On Cane Creek, deceased John Christmas, off Moccasin Creek
North Carolina		Jonathan	28-Nov	1805	12/50		48	#1731 NW of Jonathan's land
Morrow	James	Jonathan	22-Feb	1806	12/255	$1,300	508	2-tracts, South Haw-266a, other land 242acres
Morrow	Andrew	Jonathan	8-Mar	1806	12/254	$650	29	On Cain Creek
Thompson	James	Jonathan	8-Mar	1806	12/257	$800	230	Varnell's Creek
May	Ludwick	Jonathan	29-Jul	1806	12/256	$20	NA	Varnell's Creek - estate of John Campbell - deceased
Cate	James	Jonathan	6-Sep	1806	12/292	$1,200	190	Marshall Creek
Patton	James	Jonathan	22-Oct	1806	12/258	$200	370	Varnell's Creek (320a) and Dry Branch (50a)
Williams	James	Jonathan	27-Oct	1806	12/259	NA	468	Haw River - south side
Berry	Elizabeth	Jonathan	28-Oct	1806	12/260	$20	30	land of deceased Isaac Berry on great falls called Ellis Falls
Whitsman	Conrod	Jonathan	24-Jun	1809	13/222	£48.7.0	51	land on Bone Creek
Thompson	John	Jonathan	15-Nov	1809	13/282	$100	150	on Whiteheads Creek
Braxton	Hiram	Jonathan	21-Aug	1845	34/458	$5	1.5	west side of Alamance Road, N side of Mill pond by pond
McPhearson	Stephen	Joshua	22-Jan	1831	25/135	312	104	Estate of McPhearson Sarah Dixon involved Cane to Chatham line
Lochart	William	Owen	29-Nov	1796	5/774	£87.10.0	36.7	Adjacent to John McCollams plated 2/18/1788
North Carolina		Owen	8-Dec	1796	9/374	NA	200	#1422 adjacent to Owen and Ward
Hart	Stephen	Owen	5-Jan	1797	6/315	£90.0.0	60.5	William Whiteheads line called Lot #3 and #4
Findley	Hugh	Owen	30-Aug	1800	10/21	$160	25.5	adjancent to Owen and Finley's part of tract Owen lives on
Faucett	Henry	Owen	16-May	1804	12/54	$90	23	1/7 part of James Findley east Eno River
Faucett	William	Owen	26-May	1804	12/23	$90	23	another 1/7 part of James Findley east Eno River
Thompson	James	Owen	23-Apr	1810	13/350	£150.0.0	142	Eno River - James Thompson deceased land
Laughlin	Hugh	Thomas	10-Aug	1755	1/35	NA	NA	** Mill agreement **
Lyon	Richard	Thomas	9-Dec	1768	3/246	£45.0.0	70	Fred Gregg&Rich Lyon Cumberland Co. s fork Cain Creek
Austin	Solomon ETAL	Thomas	8-Mar	1794	5/98	£250.0.0	265	Little Cain Creek (see 5/189)
Holliday	Henry	Thomas	16-Jun	1796	9/96	£10.0.0	100	No location, but adjoins "Davis"
Laughlin Etal		Thomas	30-Aug	1796	9/161	£251.0.0	21	(Thomas son of William deceased) waters of Cain Creek
Clark	William	Thomas	6-Aug	1797	7/98	£350.0.0	200	Adjacent Eno River east side of Haw River
Holliday	Henry	Thomas	4-Feb	1803	10/344	£475.0.0	311	On Cain Creek
Lindley	Thomas Sr.	Thomas Jr.	11-Oct	1794	5/189	£30.0.0	265	Waters of Little Cain Creek, adj Fred Williams & Joe Weeks
Fanning	Edmond	William	2-Oct	1769	2/593	£55.0.0	21	1/2 interst in Mill (due to Laughlin death)
Morrow	James	William	22-Apr	1803	10/376	£162.10.0	200	May Creek (not sure if this was to be Mary's Creek)
North Carolina		William	4-Jan	1804	11/104		200	#1695 on Money's Creek
Carter Jr.	John	William	25-Feb	1807	12/308	$600	150	land near road to John Thompson's Mill
Campbell	Richard	William	29-Dec	1807	13/264	$600	150	payment schedule listed in this deed to 1811

Deed Records (Lindley Grantor)

From	To		Date	Year	Book	Price	Acres	Description
Lindley	Ella & A.H.	Benbow	Paris	25-Sep	1850	34/550	$1,250	62.0	Alamance Co. adj his other land and Braxton
Lindley	Grace & Owen	Findley	Hugh	3-Aug	1800	11/176	$40	5.5	Eno part of the tract Owen lives on
Lindley	James	Downing	James	25-Jul	1755	1/49	£20.0.0	100	N-side of Cane Creek adj Downing - VA currency/granville grant
Lindley	James	Faucett	James	Feb-29	1812	15/61	$40	18	Eno River
Lindley	James	Faucett	James	27-Sep	1815	16/29	$1,080	360	Both side of Eno River
Lindley	John	Lewis	Thomas	1-Feb	1781	12/33	NA	NA	Mary's Creek adj Widow Stanfield & Manors - no metes bounds
Lindley	John	Wood	Levi	4-Sep	1810	13/509	$1,250	250.0	On Rock Creek
Lindley	John	McCracken	John	17-Jun	1814	14/741	$460	230.0	McGowan's Creek
Lindley	Jonath	Foust	Mary	27-Dec	1810	14/127	$600	129.0	adjacent to Mary Foust
Lindley	Jonathan	Wilson	Edward	17-Oct	1812	26/70	$600	234.0	(Jonathan of Chatham Co.) Eno River
Lindley	Jonathan	Foust	John	22-May	1822	20/50	$250	220.0	(Jonathan of IN) Marys Creek
Lindley	Jonathan	Morrison	Robert		1790	5/326	£0.5.0	5.5	Spring Meeting House prop. Thomas willed to son Jonathan
Lindley	Jonathan	Harvey	Isaac	13-Jul	1798	14/330	$500	70.0	Land and 1/2 ownership in the Mill
Lindley	Jonathan	Marris	John	23-May	1803	10/352	$425	160.0	Varnell's Creek
Lindley	Jonathan	Holliday	Samuel	24-Feb	1804	11/143	$500	5.0	Land and 1/2 ownership in the Mill
Lindley	Jonathan	McPhearson	Enoch	21-Feb	1807	13/52	$150	37.0	adjacent to Widow Laughlin on Cane Creek
Lindley	Jonathan	Hunter	Robert	8-Jan	1810	13/405	$1,500	360.0	Land bought from Mat Hunter
Lindley	Jonathan	McPhearson	James	22-Feb	1810	13/508	$600	100.0	Cain Creek
Lindley	Jonathan	McPhearson	John	14-Apr	1810	13/508	$1,500	234.0	Cain Creek and mouth of Browns Spring branch
Lindley	Jonathan	Newlin	Nathenial	20-Apr	1810	13/417	$700	86.0	Bank of Haw River
Lindley	Jonathan	Woody	John	20-Apr	1810	13/418	$500	86.0	Bank of Haw River
Lindley	Jonathan	Davis	Thomas	1-May	1810	13/383	$2,000	16.0	Cane Creek part of Zachariah Dicks
Lindley	Jonathan	Stanford	Richard	17-May	1810	13/361	$1,500	190.0	On Cane Creek
Lindley	Jonathan	Howard	Thomas	21-May	1810	13/539	$1,400	300.0	On Cane Creek
Lindley	Jonathan	Lindley	John	2-Jun	1810	13/417	$800	348.0	McGowan's Creek
Lindley	Jonathan	Murphy	Archibald	7-Sep	1810	13/492	$1,464	393.0	West Haw River south side of Alamance
Lindley	Jonathan	McPhearson	John	28-Feb	1811	13/480	$50	7.0	Cant read the creek name
Lindley	Jonathan	Foust	Daniel	24-Apr	1811	13/539	$850	220.0	adjacent to Mary Foust & Jacob Marshall
Lindley	Jonathan	Newlin	John	27-Apr	1811	13/540	$1,300	550.0	On Mary's Creek
Lindley	Jonathan	Pennington	Levi	1-May	1811	13/538	$800	230.0	Clendinin Creek where Sam Chambers lived
Lindley	Jonathan	Lawrence	James	2-Jun	1812	14/563	$600	96.0	South side of Cane Creek land from John Brooks
Lindley	Jonathan	Braxton	William	2-Jul	1812	14/150	$300	298.0	Braxton of Chatham Co, William Lindley deceased
Lindley	Jonathan	Warren	William	20-Aug	1817	16/74	$50	50.0	Dry Branch
Lindley	Jonathan	Bobbitt	William	18-Aug	1820	18/279	$550	242.0	On Mary's Creek
Lindley	Jonathan	McDaniel	John	28-Feb	1822	18/200	$75	320.0	law suit collect debt of Luke Peacock - Verrial Creek
Lindley	Jonathan	Newlin	John	22-Apr	1822	19/366	NA	NA	Jonathan Lindley of Indiana appointing Newlin to collect debt
Lindley	Jonathan & Deborah	Stout	Joseph	13-Jan	1786	4/283	£224.0.0	120.5	N. side Cane Creek - granville grant of John Jones 1754
Lindley	Joshua	Clark	Alexander	1-Nov	1847	32/541	$512	104.0	(Josha of Chatham Co) Cane Creek
Lindley	Margaret & Thomas	Buckingham	Joseph	25-Nov	1822	21/159	Love	NA	Margaret is widow of Joe Buckinham Sr. give to her son 1/2
Lindley	Mirriam & Thomas	Crutchfield	John	20-Mar	1794	8/203	£305.0.0	65.0	Little Cain Creek adjacent to Wortham
Lindley	Owen	Whitted Jr.	William	10-Jun	1797	6/96	$251	60.0	Eno River adj to Finley (Stephen Hart former land)
Lindley	Owen	Thompson	James	23-Apr	1810	13/409	£3.10.0	120.0	West Eno River
Lindley	Owen	Lindley	James	1-Jun	1810	13/419	$1,600	403.0	Eno River plantation Owen now lives on
Lindley	Thomas	Bean	Thomas	5-Jun	1810	13/397	$1,000	200.0	Eno River willed to William Clark bu his deceased father
Lindley	Thomas	Alston	Joseph	1-May	1811	17/112	$5,000	617	On Cane Creek adjacent to mill property
Lindley	Thomas Sr.	Lindley	Thomas Jr.	11-Oct	1794	5/189	£30.0.0	265	Waters of Little Cain Creek, adj Fred Williams & Joe Weeks
Lindley	William	Lindley	Jonathan	26-Aug	1792	4/601	£80.0.0	270	Dead William's estate, part of his grant (11/17/1790)
Lindley	William	Johnston	William	27-Nov	1807	13/120	$1,800	600	Waters of the Haw
Lindley	William	Campbell	Richard	18-May	1812	14/136	$600	150	Near the road to Thompson's Mill (William is in IN)
Lindley	William	Richardson	Richie	15-Nov	1842	30/293	$550	232	On Cane Creek
Lindley	William	Zachory	Jonathan	27-Nov	1842	30/289	$650	182	on Cane Creek
Lindley	William	Benbow	Paris	17-Sep	1844	31/431	$2,300	60	Sells the Grist Mill and Land

There are many deeds listed (Grantee and Grantor deeds) that reference Mary's Creek and especially, Varnall's Creek. Here is a map showing the locations of these creeks in relation to the Haw River. Lindley's Mill (and the battle site) are off this map. If you follow Lindley Mill Road, it will be a few miles south.

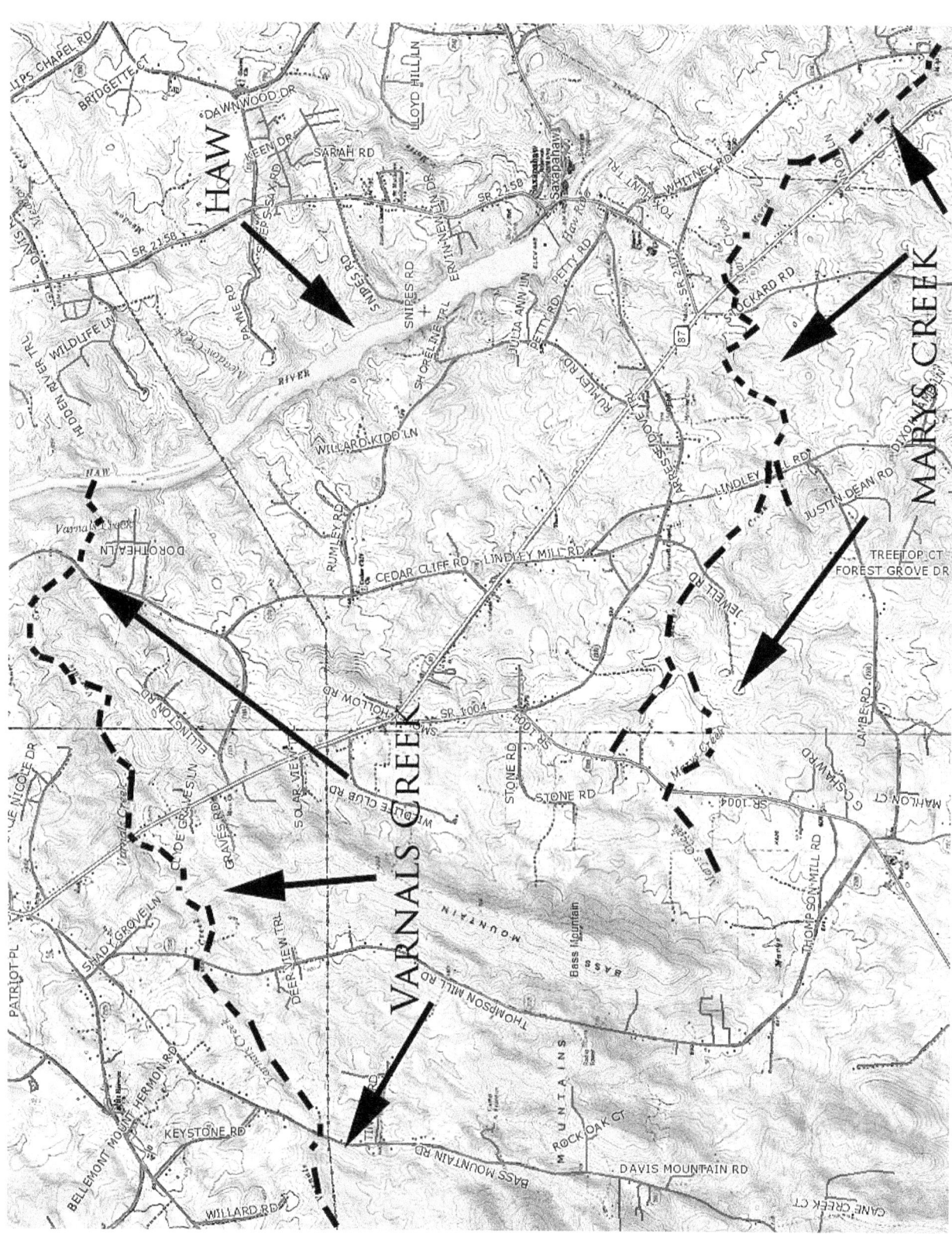

Index

Alamance County..73, 77, 81, 85, 99

Allen 19, 52, 61, 71

Allison 20, 65

Amelia County 13, 14

America 57

Armstrong 20

authority 55

Baker 47, 67

barracks 35, 65

Beatti's 19

Belford 68

Benbow 99

Benton 19, 20, 21, 24, 26, 38, 70, 73

Bladen 19, 21, 40

Braxton 5, 9, 84

British 5, 7, 10, 11, 12, 15, 19, 20, 21, 22, 23, 25, 30, 32, 35, 39, 40, 41, 43, 47, 49, 50, 51, 52, 54, 57, 60, 61, 65, 66, 67, 71, 72, 81

Broadsword 38, 71

Brown . 40, 41, 42, 43, 46, 47, 60, 66, 67

Brown Creek 42

Brown Marsh .. 41, 46, 47, 60, 66, 67

Brown Swamp 42

Brown's Ferry 44

Browning 45

Buffalo Ford 21, 71

Burke. 3, 5, 13, 17, 18, 19, 20, 21, 22, 23, 24, 25, 26, 39, 40, 41, 42, 49, 50, 51, 52, 53, 54, 55, 56, 57, 58, 59, 60, 61, 62, 64, 65

Burkes 41

Burnside 24, 68

Butler... 17, 19, 21, 22, 24, 26, 27, 29, 33, 34, 35, 38, 40, 41, 43, 45, 46, 47, 51, 53, 65, 66, 67, 71

Cain Creek. 27, 52, 68, 81, 84, 97, 100

Camden 11

Campbell 7, 41, 66

Canada 62

Cane Creek .. 7, 27, 28, 29, 30, 33, 39, 66, 81, 82, 86, 93, 99

Cape Fear River 42, 44

Captain Shubrick 55

Carolinas 11

Caruthers 19, 34, 35, 39, 41, 60

Caswell 59

Caswell Co. 66, 67

Chamber 72

Charles Town 11, 55

Charleston 50, 52

Chatham 13, 18, 41, 60, 66, 67, 81, 82, 84

Chatham County ... 41, 60, 67, 81, 82, 84

Chief Magistrate 57

chimerical 54

civil 54

Clapp 11

Clapp's 16

Clapp's Mill 16

Clendenin ... 24, 53, 65, 66, 67, 68

Cloud 38, 71

Collett 81

Colonel Stewart 36

Colonel Williams 55

Commissary 54

Company 72

Congress 56, 59

Continental.. 5, 13, 22, 23, 25, 40, 47, 54, 60, 67

Continental Army 54

Cornwallis 11

Cowpens 11

Cox's Mill 19

Craig.. 5, 7, 15, 18, 36, 40, 41, 43, 46, 47, 49, 50, 51, 54, 60, 62, 65

Cross Creek 27, 42, 66, 67, 81

Crows Ford 22

Culun Edwards 58

Cumberland County 21, 29

Dark 61

darkness 46

Darks 100

Dayton 84

debt 99

Deep River 13, 21, 38, 71

Dickins 71

Dicks 79

Digby 62

Dirks 38, 71

Dixon 99

Doctor 33, 38, 40, 71, 82

Doud 38, 71

Dr. Pyle 33, 40, 82

Duck 68

Edenton 58, 59

Edwards 19, 61, 62, 72, 83, 84

Elizabethtown 42

enemy 54, 55, 56, 57

Enoe 70

escape ...22, 23, 24, 35, 38, 39, 49, 51, 54, 55, 61, 65, 68

Eske 52

Estridge 61

Evans 79

Fanning 3, 5, 7, 12, 13, 14, 15, 17, 18, 19, 20, 21, 22, 23, 25, 26, 27, 29, 31, 32, 33, 35, 38, 39, 40, 43, 46, 50, 51, 52, 60, 61, 62, 65, 66, 67, 68, 70, 71, 79, 81, 82

Fayetteville . 27, 42, 65, 66, 67, 81

Ferguson 11

flutter wheel 100

107

Fooshee 68
ford 27, 29, 30, 31, 33, 66, 81, 100
Fraunces Tavern 57
Garrison 36
Gates 12
Gen. Greene 54, 55, 58
Gen. Leslie 54, 55
General Assembly 57
General Leslie 55, 56
Georgia 36
Governor 54, 55, 57, 59, 71
Granville 8, 17, 18, 82, 85, 86, 88, 90, 93, 97
Greene 12, 54, 55, 56, 58, 72
Grist Mill 99
Guilford 40, 64, 66, 68
Guilford Courthouse 11
guns 38, 67
Hadley 7, 79, 83
Halifax 54, 58
hanged 23, 60, 61, 79, 82
Harlet 86
Harris 79
Hart 19, 20, 24, 72
Hart's Mill 1, 2, 6, 11, 28
Haw River 7, 22, 52, 66, 71, 81, 93, 99
Hayes 58
Highland Regiment 35
Highlanders 71
Hightower 60
Hillsboro Road 100
Hillsborough ... 14, 15, 16, 17, 18, 19, 20, 21, 22, 23, 24, 25, 26, 27, 36, 38, 40, 43, 50, 52, 59, 60, 61, 62, 65, 66, 67, 68, 70, 71, 81
Hogg 23
Hogg's 38
Holloway 47, 66
Hooper 59

Horn 61
horse thief 20, 60
horses 7, 19, 25, 38, 40, 41, 46, 50
Horton 84
Huske 22, 38
Independence 57
Indiana 84
Iredell 18, 38, 40, 70
James Island 23, 50, 52, 54, 55
Jehu 84
Jones 65
Kellow 70, 71
Kettle Creek 79, 82
killed 19, 23, 24, 29, 32, 33, 35, 38, 40, 47, 51, 60, 61, 62, 65, 66, 67, 68
Kinchen 24, 52
King 11
King's Mountain 11
Kirk's Farm 19
Lambert 86
Laughlin 6, 7, 81, 83, 97, 99
Lee 72
Leslie 61
Lick Branch .... See , See
Lindley 61, 71
Lindley's Mill 11
Linley 7, 41, 61
Litterell 71
Little River 29
Livingston 41, 43, 47, 49
Livingston Creek 44
Livingston Swamp 46
Livingston's Swamp 44
loyalist 11
Loyalist .. 5, 12, 19, 20, 33, 35, 62, 82
Lucas's 46
Lumber River 19
Lutrell 38
Luttrell 35, 65, 68

Lytle 25, 50, 52, 58
Lyttle 38, 40
Maclaine 40, 59
Maddock 7
Mallett 71
Manson 46
Marion 72
Marmady 67
Martin's 35
Mary's Creek 27
May 11
McCauley 52, 61
McClennen 24
McDougal 43
McLain 29
McNeal 14, 29, 31
McNeil 20, 21, 24, 38, 40, 62, 66, 67, 68, 71
McRae 39
Mebane 21, 24, 33, 34, 35, 38, 41, 44, 47, 52, 60, 65, 66, 67, 71
medicine 41
medicines 40
Meeting House 30, 83
Merchant Mill 99
Military 55
militia ... 12, 18, 23, 25, 46, 49, 66, 67
Mill 71
mill race 100
Mitchell 44
Moor's Creek Bridge 35
Moore 41, 44, 46, 65, 66, 67
Morton 79
Mountflorence 20
Mouzon 81
Musgrove Mill 11
Nall 65
Nalls 71
Nash 59
Navy 11

108

Nelson ... 71
New Brunswick ... 62
New Hope ... 61
New Jersey ... 57
New York ... 57
New York City ... 57
night ... 21, 22, 24, 26, 27, 39, 40, 44, 46, 47, 65, 66, 68
North Carolina 10, 11, 12, 54, 64
Nova Scotia ... 36, 62
Nutbush Church ... 17
O'Neal ... 40, 51, 66
officers ... 71
Orange County ... 5, 7, 14, 19, 24, 47, 51, 60, 66, 70, 73, 81, 82, 85, 99
Parliament ... 62
parole ... 49, 50, 54
Patterson ... 67
Perry ... 99
Piedmont ... 81
Pile ... 71
pit ... 35, 65
plunder ... 38, 40
plundering ... 38
Porterfield ... 70
preliminary peace treaty ... 57
prisoner of war ... 35
prisoners ... 54, 57
PRO ... 18, 35, 40
Proclamation ... 57
Pyle 11, 33, 40, 41, 64, 79, 81, 82, 84
Pyle Jr ... 82
Pyle's ... 82
Pyle's Defeat ... 82
Pyles Defeat ... 11
Quaker Meeting House ... 27
Race to the Dan ... 11

Raft Swamp ... 39, 43
Ramsay's Mills ... 38
Ramsey Mill ... 65
Ramsey's Mill ... 19
Randolph ... 13, 18, 19
Ray ... 43, 62
Read ... 38
Rebel ... 21, 36
rebels ... 11, 23, 27, 29, 46
Regulators ... 70, 81
Renolds ... 66, 67
Ricketts ... 61
rifling ... 38
Robeson ... 47
Rochester ... 72
Rosser ... 67
Ruth Hadley ... 7
Rutherford ... 60, 66, 67
Samuel Johnston ... 58
Sanders ... 66
saw mill ... 99
Saw Mill ... 99
scoundrels ... 59
servants ... 50
shot ... 72
skull ... 35, 67, 68
Smith ... 33, 60, 67, 68
South Carolina ... 11
Spain ... 57
Spring Meeting ... 9, 30, 35, 81, 83
Spring Meeting House ... 9, 30
St. Augustine ... 62
Stafford Creek ... 29, 30, 31, 33
Stallion ... 7, 41
State ... 54, 55, 57
Stevens ... 47
Stewart ... 1, 2, 5, 35, 64
Sullivan's Island ... 50

surgeons ... 40
Sutphin ... 99
Tarleton ... 11, 12
Tatum ... 20, 40
Taylor ... 71
Terrell's Creek ... 88, 90
Thomas ... 23
Thomas Lindley ... 6, 7, 9
Thompson ... 65, 99
Tinnens ... 71
Tories ... 5, 12, 20, 22, 23, 24, 26, 28, 30, 31, 32, 35, 38, 40, 41, 45, 47, 49, 52, 60, 65, 66, 67, 68, 71, 81
Tory ... 5, 7, 11, 12, 21, 50, 60, 62, 65, 66, 68, 79, 82
Treaty of Paris ... 57
Trousdale ... 66
Tryon ... 14, 70, 81
villains ... 59
violation ... 54
Virginia ... 10, 11, 13, 14, 24
wagon ... 71
Walter Brown ... 47
war ... 57
Waxhaws ... 11
Weitzel's Mill ... 11
White ... 67, 79, 83
Williams ... 18, 46
Williamsboro ... 17
Wilmington ... 3, 7, 11, 13, 15, 18, 19, 20, 21, 24, 27, 36, 39, 42, 44, 45, 46, 47, 49, 50, 52, 53, 54, 65, 66, 67, 71, 81
Woody's Ferry ... 27, 52, 81
wounds ... 7, 33, 35, 67
Yorktown ... 11
Young ... 19